THE BEGINNER'S GUIDE TO STOICISM

EMBRACE ANCIENT WISDOM TO OVERCOME MODERN STRESS AND ANXIETY

ADRIAN COLE

CONTENTS

INTRODUCTION

Have you ever felt overwhelmed by the chaos of modern life, unsure of how to find peace amidst the noise? If so, you are not alone. Stress, anxiety, and a pervasive sense of dissatisfaction frequently punctuate our daily existence. However, what if I told you that an ancient philosophy could offer you the tools to cope and thrive in today's world?

Stoicism is a school of philosophy that dates back to ancient Greece and Rome. It focuses on building resilience, finding inner peace, and controlling one's reactions to external events. It teaches us that while we cannot control every aspect of our lives, we can control our sensitivities to them, which in turn can dramatically improve our well-being.

My journey with Stoicism began with skepticism. As someone deep-rooted in the challenges of modern life, I initially doubted how knowledge from thousands of years ago could ease my contemporary woes. However, through trial and error, I discovered not only the practicality of Stoic principles but also their profound effect on my mental health and overall happiness.

This book aims to clarify Stoicism for beginners, as it guides you through the basic concepts of Stoic philosophy and provides you with manageable phases to integrate its wisdom into your everyday life. You don't need a background in philosophy to begin —just an open mind and willingness to explore how these ancient concepts can address modern problems.

You, the reader, are probably an adult seeking a reliable and philosophical approach to personal growth and stress management. Perhaps you've noticed Stoicism's growing popularity in discussions about mental health and well-being and are curious about how to apply it to your own life. This book is for those intrigued by the practical benefits of a philosophical life.

In the following chapters, we will explore the core beliefs of Stoicism, examine the lives of notable Stoic thinkers, and provide practical exercises that you can implement immediately. Each part of the book builds on the previous one, creating a comprehensive roadmap from theory to practice.

This book combines historical insights, practical exercises, personal anecdotes, and practical research to ensure a well-rounded and engaging learning experience. By blending these elements, I aim to make Stoicism not only relatable but also proven in its effectiveness in improving your life.

By the end of this book, you won't just understand Stoicism; you will have started living it, finding in its ancient wisdom a path to a more serene and resilient life. Embrace this journey of transformation, where you will equip yourself with enduring Stoic strategies to navigate the complexities of modern life with clarity and resilience.

1

LAYING THE FOUNDATIONS OF STOICISM

At the heart of every philosophy lies the promise of a better way to live, a plan for navigating the complexities of living with a steadier hand and a more serene mind. Stoicism, perhaps more than any other ancient philosophy, extends this promise not through abstract theorization but through practical, easy-to-understand wisdom. As we explore this philosophical giant, it's vital to understand that Stoicism isn't just about enduring hardship—it's about transforming our reactions to hardships, thus changing our lives for the better.

Some of the most influential figures in history, including George Washington and Thomas Jefferson, drew deeply on Stoic principles to guide their decisions. This timeless appeal underscores the adaptability and enduring relevance of Stoicism, making it as appropriate in the bustling streets of today's metropolises as it was in ancient marketplaces.

WHAT IS STOICISM? UNDERSTANDING ITS ORIGINS AND CORE BELIEFS

Defining Stoicism

Stoicism is a school of classical Greek philosophy that began in Athens with Zeno of Citium around 300 BC and continued throughout the Roman and Greek world until approximately the 3rd century AD. It is more than just a set of beliefs; it is a way of life that emphasizes ethics, the discipline of the will, and the logic of the natural world. The Stoics focused on practicality—an aspect that made this philosophy accessible and practical for both scholars and common people in ancient times.

Built on the foundation of understanding what we can control and what we cannot, the central aim of the Stoic doctrine is to achieve a state of inner peace and resilience, regardless of external circumstances, by mastering one's own emotions and actions. This core principle helps individuals focus their energy and attention on their actions and attitudes, which are in their power to change, rather than external events that are not.

The Core Beliefs of Stoicism

At the core of Stoic philosophy are several fundamental beliefs: the logic of the universe, the discipline of desire, and the acceptance of fate, all of which govern emotional responses. Stoics believe that by understanding the nature of the world and our place within it, we can learn to accept the moment as it presents itself, respond with reason rather than emotion, and, therefore, maintain tranquility.

Stoics endeavor to live in harmony with nature, acknowledge that everything is interconnected, and that human reasoning is part of the divine intellect. This alignment with nature involves not only gratefulness for the natural world but also an understanding of life's ebb and flow, accepting both successes and failures with calmness. Stoicism teaches that distress comes not from events themselves but from our feelings about them, a viewpoint that empowers individuals to cultivate inner strength and flexibility.

Historical Context

The historical and social contexts of the Hellenistic period, marked by warfare, political upheaval, and cultural shifts, significantly influenced the development of Stoicism. This era saw the shattering of Alexander the Great's empire and the rise of the Roman Empire, both times of momentous uncertainty and change. Stoicism offered a sense of calm and stability, proposing that despite external chaos, individuals could achieve inner peace through self-control and rational thinking.

Stoicism's strength and pragmatism were further consolidated as it spread to Rome, where thinkers such as Seneca, Epictetus, and Marcus Aurelius adapted its principles to guide leadership, governance, and personal conduct amidst the complexities of empire.

Connecting to Modern Relevance

The principles of Stoicism have found a new connection to today's fast-paced, high-stress environments. The Stoic focus on controlling one's reactions to peripheral events reflects the challenges faced by modern individuals dealing with the pressures of daily life. In an age where anxiety and external pressures are rife, the Stoic practice of focusing on what is within our personal control—

our thoughts, behaviors, and reactions—delivers a powerful tool for managing stress and enhancing satisfaction in our lives.

Through Stoicism, you can learn to detach from the chaos that surrounds you, approach life's challenges with a calm mind, and respond to every situation with thoughtfulness and integrity. In embracing these principles, you engage in a proven strategy that has supported individuals through tumultuous times for centuries, offering not just a philosophy of endurance but a path to thriving no matter what life throws your way.

THE ART OF DIFFERENTIATING BETWEEN CONTROL AND SURRENDER

One of the most transformative aspects of Stoicism involves understanding and applying the Dichotomy of Control, a principle that succinctly divides the elements of our lives into two clear categories: those we can control and those we cannot. This principle, at its core, teaches that our thoughts and actions fall within our sphere of control, while external events and the actions of others do not. By internalizing this distinction, we not only enhance our ability to cope with life's challenges but also set the stage for genuine personal growth and increased satisfaction.

Consider a typical day: you might get stuck in traffic, have a disagreement with a colleague, or face unexpected delays in a planned project. In each scenario, the Stoic practice would involve identifying elements you can control—your responses and actions —and recognizing those you cannot, such as the behavior of other drivers, your colleague's opinions, or the timing of external approvals. This differentiation is crucial because it shifts the focus from frustration over uncontrollable outcomes to proactive management of your reactions and choices. For instance, while you cannot clear the traffic, you can choose to listen to a podcast or an audiobook, transforming a stressful commute into a productive or enjoyable time. In the workplace, rather than stewing over a disagreement, you could decide to articulate your viewpoints clearly and seek common ground, thereby fostering a collaborative rather than confrontational atmosphere.

To practically apply this concept in daily life, consider maintaining a daily journal. Each evening, reflect on the day's events, categorizing them as 'within my control' and 'beyond my control.' This exercise not only aids in reinforcing the Stoic dichotomy but also cultivates a habit of mindful reflection. You might write about the traffic and note your decision to engage in a more rewarding activity, thus focusing on your control over your reaction rather than the external situation. Over time, this practice boosts a shift in perspective, where you naturally begin to engage more with your sphere of influence and less with the uncontrollable.

The psychological benefits of this Stoic practice are profound—engaging consistently with what we can control while surrendering to what we can't leads to a significant reduction in anxiety and stress. This is mainly because much of our societal anxiety stems from a perceived lack of control over external events. When we realign our focus towards areas where we have genuine influence, such as our personal efforts and attitudes, we feel not only more empowered but also more peaceful. This empowerment fosters a proactive attitude toward life; rather than being reactive to situations, we become active participants in shaping our own well-being.

Moreover, integrating the Dichotomy of Control into your life equips you to handle adversity with superior calm and resilience. When faced with professional setbacks or personal trials, a Stoic approach prompts you to assess which aspects of a situation you can influence. If a project at work is criticized, instead of harboring resentment or doubt, you might choose to seek constructive feedback and focus on improving your skills, thus converting potential negative energy into a catalyst for personal and professional development. This mindset, rooted in Stoicism, transforms challenges into prospects for growth, ensuring that you keep your composure and purpose regardless of outside pressures.

Embracing the Dichotomy of Control is fundamentally about nurturing a deep sense of inner stability and self-assurance. It teaches us that while we may not always have control over the events that develop around us, we hold the final authority over how we respond. This is empowering, placing the reins of our emotional and mental well-being firmly in our hands. As you continue to practice this Stoic principle, you will notice a shift not only in your reactions but in your overall approach to life—a shift towards a more deliberate, thoughtful, and resilient life, not grounded in the chaos of the outside world but in the clarity of your rational choices.

EXPLORING THE STOIC VIRTUES: WISDOM, COURAGE, JUSTICE, AND TEMPERANCE

The Stoic philosophy is built on a foundation of virtues that guide the ethical range of its followers—Wisdom, Courage, Justice, and Temperance. Each of these fundamental virtues is not only a trait to be developed in isolation but is interrelated, supporting and enhancing each other in the cultivation of a balanced and principled life.

Defining the Cardinal Virtues

Wisdom in Stoicism is regarded as both practical and philosophical knowledge. It involves the ability to navigate complex situations with clarity and ethical insight, distinguishing between good, bad, and indifferent actions based on their true nature and potential consequences. Courage goes beyond physical bravery to encompass moral and psychological resilience—the strength and integrity to face internal conflicts, ethical dilemmas, and life's unavoidable sufferings. Justice comprises the fair treatment of others, rooted in kindness, social responsibility, and community service, while recognizing the inherent value of all human beings and striving to act in ways that benefit both the individual and the community. Temperance is the practice of self-control and moderation, guiding one to make choices not determined by passions or desires but aligned with one's best logical interests.

Connecting Virtues to Daily Life

In the daily grind, these virtues translate into actions and decisions that shape the quality of our lives and our interactions with others. Consider a professional setting: applying Wisdom might involve choosing the most effective and ethical approach to a complex project and recognizing the long-term impacts over short-term gains. Courage is called upon when we must speak up about workplace issues or advocate for changes that align with our moral values despite potential opposition or risk. Justice is practiced through fairness in dealings with colleagues, ensuring that everyone's contributions are acknowledged and valued and that decisions are made with consideration for their effects on all stakeholders. Temperance manifests in managing our ambitions and work-life balance, ensuring that our pursuit of professional success does not compromise our health or personal relationships.

At home or in personal settings, these virtues are equally vital. Wisdom guides parents when imparting ethical values to their children. Courage enables individuals to confront personal fears or challenges, perhaps addressing long-standing personal issues or making significant life changes that, while daunting, promise substantial personal growth. Justice plays a role in how one contributes to one's community, perhaps through volunteer work or advocacy, while Temperance can help one manage personal finances and resist the lure of indulgences that might lead to harm.

Highlighting the Interconnection of Virtues

The development of one virtue often aids the enhancement of others. For instance, true Courage is not reckless but is guided by Wisdom, which assesses risks and determines the worthiness of a cause. Justice is informed by Courage, as it often requires bravery to ensure fairness and equitable treatment in the face of societal pressures. Similarly, Temperance can prevent the pursuit of justice from turning into zealotry, reminding us to seek balanced solutions that benefit the broadest community. This interplay ensures that the practice of one virtue reinforces and elevates the others, promoting a well-rounded approach to personal and moral development.

Encouraging Self-Assessment

Understanding and developing these virtues starts with self-assessment, which involves honest reflection on one's current strengths and areas for growth. You might find yourself naturally aligned with Justice, perhaps easily engaging in community service or advocacy, yet struggle with Temperance, finding it difficult to say no or to moderate desires that lead to excess. By identifying these natural inclinations and areas of challenge, you can focus your efforts on cultivating balance, ensuring that no virtue is left underdeveloped.

Engaging in regular self-reflection can be facilitated by keeping a virtue journal, where daily or weekly entries focus on actions taken, decisions made, and their alignment with Stoic virtues. Such a practice not only enhances self-awareness but also encourages proactive living that consistently aligns with Stoic ideals. Over time, this reflective practice can deepen your understanding of how these virtues operate in your life and how you can consciously integrate them into your daily actions and broader life decisions.

In essence, the Stoic virtues offer a framework for living that promotes not only personal well-being but also the welfare of others, creating a ripple effect that extends from individual actions to collective harmony. By striving to embody wisdom, courage, justice, and temperance in all aspects of life, we engage in a continuous process of ethical refinement and personal growth that is both challenging and deeply rewarding.

EUDAIMONIA: THE STOIC CONCEPTION OF A FLOURISHING LIFE

At the heart of Stoic philosophy lies the pursuit of Eudaimonia, a term that resonates deeply through the ages, embodying the highest human good. But what exactly is Eudaimonia? In its simplest translation, it means 'flourishing' or 'happiness'; however, in the Stoic context, it denotes a quality of life achieved through the cultivation of virtue and rational living. Unlike the fleeting pleasures sought in hedonistic pursuits, which are often dependent on external circumstances and can lead to ephemeral satisfaction, Eudaimonia represents a state of enduring well-being that emanates from a life lived in harmony with one's rational nature.

The distinction between common notions of happiness and Stoic happiness is crucial and profoundly liberating. While contempo-

rary society often equates happiness with external success—
wealth, popularity, and luxury—Stoicism invites us to shift our
focus inward. It teaches that true happiness is found not in
external acquisitions or sensory pleasures but in developing the
inner virtues—wisdom, courage, justice, and temperance. This
form of happiness is stable and sustainable because life's inevitable
challenges and changes do not easily disrupt it.

Achieving Eudaimonia requires more than intellectual understanding; it necessitates practical engagement with life's daily
demands through a Stoic lens, which involves consistent reflection
on one's actions, ensuring they align with personal and moral
values. For instance, consider the practice of journaling, a method
embraced by many Stoics, both ancient and modern, as a way to
reflect on one's daily experiences and evaluate them against Stoic
principles. This habit encourages mindfulness and self-correction,
fostering a life that not only espouses virtue but actively practices
it.

Moreover, aligning life with one's values in the Stoic sense means
prioritizing actions and choices that enhance personal virtue and
contribute to the common good. It involves asking oneself regularly, "Is this action just? Does this decision support my growth in
temperance? Am I exercising courage in this challenge?" Such
questions guide the Stoic practitioner towards actions that are not
only personally beneficial but also socially responsible, thus
expanding the scope of Eudaimonia to include the well-being of
the community and relationships.

Historical and contemporary anecdotes abound with examples of
individuals achieving Eudaimonia despite challenging circumstances. Consider the case of Admiral James Stockdale, who was
held captive during the Vietnam War. Stockdale credited his
survival and resilience to the principles of Stoicism, particularly

the works of Epictetus, which he had studied prior to his capture. His ordeal included severe hardship and uncertainty, yet his commitment to Stoic principles provided a framework for maintaining mental clarity, moral integrity, and, ultimately, a profound sense of personal fulfillment, even in captivity. His experience underscores the Stoic belief that external conditions do not define our happiness or our capacity to live a fulfilling life.

In more everyday contexts, consider a professional who practices Stoicism in the midst of a volatile career in a high-stress environment. By focusing on maintaining integrity, using rational judgment, and managing personal reactions to workplace dynamics, this individual cultivates a professional life that not only achieves the external metrics of success but also maintains internal peace and ethical standards, thus embodying the Stoic ideal of Eudaimonia.

Embracing community and relationships is also vital in the pursuit of Eudaimonia. Stoicism teaches that humans are inherently social creatures, and our well-being is deeply connected to that of others. Engaging positively with our communities—whether offering support during difficult times, participating in community-building activities, or fostering environments of mutual respect and understanding—enhances our sense of connection and shared humanity. This engagement not only enriches our own lives but also reaffirms our commitment to the Stoic principles of justice and fairness, fostering a broader social environment where Eudaimonia can flourish.

Thus, the path to Eudaimonia is not a solitary trek but a dynamic interaction with the world, guided by rational principles and a commitment to virtue. It is a state continuously cultivated through thoughtful actions, reflective practices, and meaningful engagements with others. In this way, Stoicism offers not just a philosophical view of happiness but a robust, practical framework for living well. Whether facing adversity or celebrating success, the Stoic pursuit of Eudaimonia provides a steadfast compass, ensuring that every aspect of life is approached with wisdom, integrity, and a deep-seated tranquility that comes from living in alignment with one's deepest values.

THE STOIC PHILOSOPHERS: LIVES AND LESSONS

As we delve deeper into the essence of Stoicism, it becomes evident that the lives of its philosophers are as instructive as their teachings. Among these venerable figures, Seneca stands out not only for his philosophical insights but for his tumultuous life, which serves as a profound lesson in resilience and inner peace. His experiences, fraught with political intrigue and personal hardship, paired with his thoughtful writings, offer a rich source of guidance for anyone facing the vicissitudes of modern life.

SENECA'S INSIGHTS ON RESILIENCE AND INNER PEACE

Seneca's Personal Challenges

Lucius Annaeus Seneca, commonly known as Seneca the Younger, navigated a life replete with extremes of wealth and deprivation, power and peril. His career in the complex and often perilous world of Roman politics saw him rising to the height of influence as an advisor to Emperor Nero, only to be cast into exile in Corsica under Claudius. This exile, prompted by accusations of an affair with Caligula's sister, was a period of profound personal suffering and introspection for Seneca. Yet, it was also during this time that he composed some of his most poignant works on Stoicism, reflecting on the nature of adversity and the human condition. His eventual return to Rome and subsequent rise to power did little to secure his safety, as he later faced forced suicide by the increasingly paranoid Nero. Through all these fluctuations of fortune, Senecas's writings and actions reflected a deep commitment to Stoic principles, emphasizing resilience, ethical integrity, and the pursuit of tranquility amidst turmoil.

Teachings on Resilience

Seneca's writings, rich with personal reflections on his own experiences, offer timeless insights into the cultivation of resilience. In his moral essays and letters, he frequently discusses the importance of resilience in the face of adversity, advocating for a perspective that views obstacles not merely as misfortunes but as opportunities for growth and affirmation of character. For instance, in his *Letters from a Stoic*, Seneca advises, "The bravest sight in the world is to see a great man struggling against adversity." His letters to his friends and political contemporaries are replete with advice on maintaining composure and integrity no matter the external circumstances. He teaches that true resilience stems not from avoiding adversity but from engaging with challenges in ways that refine and affirm one's virtues.

Modern Application of Seneca's Resilience

In today's context, Seneca's thoughts on resilience have profound implications, especially when dealing with professional setbacks or personal losses. Imagine facing a sudden career setback, such as a project failure or job loss. Applying Seneca's principles, you would focus not on the loss itself but on your response to it. This might involve viewing the setback as a chance to reassess your career path, develop new skills, or strengthen your professional network. Similarly, in the face of personal loss, Seneca's advice would guide you to seek consolation in the acceptance of life's impermanence and to find peace by cherishing memories and lessons learned from loved ones.

The Role of Inner Peace

For Seneca, resilience is linked intricately to the achievement of inner peace. He postulates that true peace comes from within and is not disturbed by external chaos. In his view, one can achieve inner peace through the acceptance of fate and the understanding that suffering and hardship are part of the human experience. This acceptance is not passive resignation but an active, rational acknowledgment that enables one to maintain composure and clarity of thought in any situation. For Seneca, the cultivation of inner peace involves a daily practice of reflection, self-examination, and deliberate choice to respond to life's challenges with equanimity and reason.

Visualization Exercise: Finding Your Stoic Center

To integrate Seneca's teachings into your life, try this simple visualization exercise. Find a quiet place and take a few deep breaths to center yourself. Visualize a recent event that caused you distress. Now, reimagine the event from a Stoic perspective, focusing on your control over your response rather than the event itself. Ask yourself what virtues you can apply to this scenario, such as patience, courage, or wisdom. Reflect on how changing your response could change the outcome, both externally and internally. This exercise can help you cultivate a more resilient and peaceful approach to the challenges you face.

Through his life and writings, Seneca provides a compelling example of how Stoic philosophy can be lived out, even in the face of extreme adversity. His insights into resilience and inner peace offer valuable guidance for navigating the intricacies of modern life, teaching us that by focusing on our internal responses and cultivating tranquility, we can face any circumstance with clarity and strength.

MARCUS AURELIUS: A DAY IN THE LIFE OF A STOIC EMPEROR

Imagine the sun rising over the ancient city of Rome, its first light casting long shadows behind the marble columns of the Imperial Palace. It is here that we find Marcus Aurelius, not only the ruler of a vast empire but also a devoted Stoic, weaving the principles of this philosophy into the very fabric of his daily life. His days, rigorously structured yet reflective, serve as a profound example of how Stoicism can infuse one's duties with wisdom, balance, and ethical rigor.

Marcus Aurelius's mornings would likely begin before dawn, a time reserved for solitude and the first of his meditative practices. Here, in the quiet predawn hours, the emperor reflected on the day ahead, mentally preparing himself to meet his responsibilities not just as a ruler but as a Stoic. These moments of reflection were crucial, allowing him to align his actions with his values, ensuring that each decision was made not in pursuit of personal glory but for the greater good of his people. His commitment to Stoicism profoundly influenced his approach to governance, emphasizing justice, temperance, and the welfare of others above the easy temptations of power and luxury.

Duties of state consumed the bulk of his day—meetings with military leaders, discussions with advisors, and the endless adjudication of disputes. Yet, even amidst this whirlwind of activity, Marcus Aurelius remained a philosopher at heart. His Stoic viewpoint was evident in his measured responses and the deliberate pace he engaged with each issue, embodying the Stoic ideal of thoughtful deliberation. He often reminded himself and those around him that the role of a leader is to serve, a concept deeply rooted in Stoic ethics. Each decision, each law passed, and each conflict resolved were seen through the lens of how they served the common welfare, reflecting his unwavering commitment to justice and virtue.

Marcus Aurelius's Meditative Practices

Integral to Marcus Aurelius's daily routine were his meditative practices, which were not only personal reflections but also formed the basis of his writings in *Meditations*. These writings, a series of personal notes, thoughts, and reminders, offer a window into his soul, revealing a man who sought wisdom and virtue in every aspect of his life. *Meditations* is not a philosophical treatise but a personal journal filled with his struggles, insights, and resolutions. In passages where he writes about accepting the things he cannot change or focusing on his improvements rather than criticizing others, we see his commitment to Stoic principles, such as the dichotomy of control and the importance of self-mastery.

These meditations were likely penned during quieter moments, perhaps in the evening, as he reflected on the events that had transpired during the day. They served as a kind of self-dialogue, a way for Marcus Aurelius to counsel himself to stay true to his Stoic path amidst the immense pressures of Imperial life. His writings emphasize the importance of self-reflection, a practice that allowed him to remain grounded and maintain inner peace despite the external chaos of political life.

Leadership Lessons from Marcus Aurelius

The leadership style of Marcus Aurelius, heavily influenced by his Stoic beliefs, offers timeless lessons in ethical and effective governance. His reign, often marked by fairness and a genuine concern for the well-being of his subjects, stands in stark contrast to the frequently tyrannical rule seen in other Roman emperors. His approach underscores the Stoic belief that power should be exercised with responsibility and restraint and that the measure of a true leader is not the extent of their power but how they use it to benefit others.

Modern leaders can draw significant insights from his example, particularly in the realms of business and politics, where ethical challenges are rampant. Marcus Aurelius's emphasis on virtue and integrity in leadership, his focus on serving rather than ruling, and his commitment to personal ethical development are principles that can profoundly influence contemporary leadership practices. In a world where leaders are often swayed by personal ambition or external pressures, the Stoic model advocated by Marcus Aurelius offers a compelling alternative, promoting a leadership style that is both morally grounded and effective.

Examining His Legacy

The legacy of Marcus Aurelius extends far beyond his reign as emperor. His life and writings have influenced countless individuals across the centuries, reinforcing his status not only as a political figure but as a philosopher-king. His embodiment of Stoic principles, particularly under the strain of Imperial responsibilities, offers a powerful example of how philosophy can be lived in practice, not just contemplated in theory.

His impact on Roman society was profound, instilling values of justice, temperance, and rationality at a time when such qualities were often overshadowed by corruption and decadence. Moreover, his writings in *Meditations* have endured as one of the most precise expressions of Stoic philosophy, providing guidance and inspiration to those seeking to understand and implement Stoic principles in their lives. Through his example, Marcus Aurelius remains a beacon of how one can wield great power with great responsibility, guided by the wisdom of Stoic philosophy. His life reminds us that the true test of our principles is not how we wield them in tranquility but how we hold to them in times of adversity.

EPICTETUS ON FREEDOM AND THE ILLUSION OF CONTROL

Epictetus, whose origins starkly contrast with the philosophical stature he eventually attained, offers one of the most compelling narratives in Stoic philosophy. Born into slavery in the Roman Empire, Epictetus's early life was marked by limitations and hardships that anyone might assume would constrain his spirit. However, his journey from being a slave to a revered Stoic teacher underscores a fundamental Stoic belief: true freedom is a state of mind, not a physical condition. This belief shaped his teachings, which profoundly influenced not only his contemporaries but also countless individuals across centuries.

Epictetus's philosophy centers on the dichotomy of control, a concept that he spoke of with profound clarity and simplicity. He taught us that understanding what we can control and what we cannot is the first step toward freedom. In his discourses, he famously stated, "Some things are in our control and others not." The things in our control are our opinions, aspirations, desires, and the things that repel us. These areas are where we have real power. In contrast, things we cannot control include our bodies, possessions, reputation, and social status—elements that are often mistakenly viewed as sources of freedom or power.

This teaching is revolutionary because it shifts the focus from external acquisitions or conditions to internal strength and resilience. For Epictetus, the essence of freedom lies in mastering one's internal state, cultivating virtues, and responding to external events with wisdom and equanimity. This perspective is incredibly empowering, suggesting that regardless of one's external circumstances—whether one is a CEO, a middle manager, or a recent graduate entering the workforce—the capacity for personal freedom and effectiveness lies fundamentally within.

Applying Epictetus's ideas on freedom and control can profoundly impact how individuals navigate both personal and professional challenges today. In the professional realm, consider the scenario of facing an unexpected layoff or substantial organizational changes—situations typically loaded with uncertainty and stress. Rather than being consumed by the anxiety of the unknown or fixating on the instability, you can apply Epictetus's teachings by focusing on your response to the change. This might involve proactively seeking new opportunities, enhancing your skills, or even reassessing your career path to align more closely with your core values and interests. By focusing on these areas—clearly within your control—you not only maintain a sense of personal agency but will also turn potential adversity into a catalyst for growth.

In your personal life, Epictetus's philosophy can be equally transformative. Consider personal relationships, which often involve complexities that can lead to frustration or unhappiness. Epictetus would advise focusing on your individual actions and reactions—elements you can control—rather than attempting to change the other person. This approach fosters healthier relationships built on understanding and respect for personal boundaries rather than conflict and the futile desire to control others.

The implications of Epictetus's teachings for personal empowerment are profound. His life is a testament to the idea that external conditions do not define us; instead, our internal responses to those conditions shape our freedom and happiness. This perspective encourages a proactive approach to life, where challenges are seen not as barriers but as opportunities to reinforce and express our values and virtues. It teaches that personal empowerment stems from mental discipline and philosophical insight—qualities that enable us to navigate life's changes with confidence and poise.

Epictetus's narrative and teachings continue to resonate because they address a universal quest for freedom and happiness—a quest that is as pertinent today as it was in ancient times. His emphasis on internal control, coupled with the practical strategies he proposes, provides a robust framework for living a fulfilled and free life, regardless of external circumstances. By internalizing and applying these principles, you can cultivate a resilient and empowered approach to both personal and professional challenges, embodying the true spirit of Stoic freedom.

MODERN STOICS: HOW TODAY'S THINKERS APPLY ANCIENT WISDOM

The resurgence of Stoicism in contemporary society is not merely a revival but a vibrant reinvention, adapting ancient wisdom to suit the needs and challenges of the modern world. Today, a diverse array of philosophers, writers, and thought leaders have embraced Stoic principles, infusing them into their work and daily lives. These modern Stoics not only interpret Stoic philosophy for today's audience but also actively demonstrate its relevance and applicability across various fields.

One notable figure in the realm of modern Stoicism is Ryan Holiday, whose works such as *The Obstacle Is the Way* and *Daily Stoic* have introduced Stoic philosophy to a broad audience, emphasizing its usefulness in overcoming personal and professional challenges. Holiday's writings distill complex Stoic concepts into actionable advice, making them accessible and applicable to readers worldwide. His approach underscores the Stoic belief that obstacles are not impediments but opportunities for growth, a message that resonates deeply in today's fast-paced, challenge-laden world.

Similarly, Massimo Pigliucci, a philosopher and author of *How to Be a Stoic*, embodies the practical application of Stoicism through his blend of personal anecdotes and philosophical discourse. Pigliucci explores the ethical and practical dimensions of Stoicism and encourages readers to live a more thoughtful and reflective life. His work not only elaborates on the theoretical aspects of Stoicism but also provides concrete examples of how to apply these principles in everyday situations, from handling stress at work to managing personal relationships.

The influence of Stoicism is also evident in the field of psychology, particularly in the development of cognitive-behavioral therapy (CBT), which shares many principles with Stoic thought. The work of Donald Robertson, a cognitive-behavioral therapist and author of *The Philosophy of CBT*, illustrates how to integrate Stoic techniques for managing thoughts and emotions into modern therapeutic practices. Robertson's integration of philosophy and psychology demonstrates the adaptability of Stoic ideas, proving that they can provide robust frameworks for mental health and well-being in the 21st century.

In the business world, Stoicism has been adopted by leaders and entrepreneurs who use its teachings to foster resilience, ethical leadership, and a balanced approach to success. Tim Ferriss, an entrepreneur and author, frequently discusses the impact of Stoicism on his approach to business and personal productivity. By advocating for practices such as the "fear-setting" exercise—which involves defining and confronting fears to overcome procrastination and take calculated risks—Ferriss showcases how to effectively utilize Stoic principles to achieve professional success and personal fulfillment.

The global Stoic community has seen significant growth, facilitated by the rise of digital platforms and social media. Online forums, blogs, and virtual conferences have allowed individuals from various parts of the world to connect, share experiences, and learn from each other, fostering a sense of global connection and shared human experience. These communities provide a space for ongoing dialogue and collaboration, ensuring that Stoic philosophy remains a living, evolving tradition. Through podcasts, interactive webinars, and online courses, modern Stoics continue to explore and expand the boundaries of Stoic philosophy, making it relevant to diverse audiences and contemporary issues.

As Stoicism continues to inspire and influence people around the world, it is clear that this ancient philosophy retains its power and relevance. Its principles of resilience, rationality, and virtue offer timeless solutions to modern problems, providing individuals and communities with the tools they need to lead more thoughtful, productive, and meaningful lives. The work of modern Stoics not only preserves the legacy of ancient thinkers like Marcus Aurelius and Seneca but also enriches it, proving that Stoic wisdom is not confined to the past but is a living, breathing guide to living well in the present.

As we close this exploration of modern Stoicism, it is evident that the echoes of ancient Stoic thought continue to resonate through time, adapted by contemporary voices into a robust framework for living in today's complex world. The lessons drawn from both historical and modern Stoics provide us with invaluable insights into the art of living, emphasizing that true contentment and success are achieved not through external achievements but through the cultivation of virtue, resilience, and rationality.

In the next chapter, we will delve into practical Stoicism, examining specific tools and techniques that you can apply in your everyday life to harness the full potential of Stoic philosophy. Join us as we explore how to turn philosophical insights into everyday actions, bringing Stoicism into the heart of your daily experiences and interactions.

PRACTICAL STOICISM: TOOLS FOR TODAY

In the hustle of everyday life, where decisions loom large from the moment you sip your morning coffee to when you switch off the bedside lamp, how do you ensure that your choices are not just reactive but reflective and aligned with your deepest values? This is where Stoicism, far from being a dusty relic of the past, strides into the contemporary arena with clarity and purpose. It offers not just a way of understanding the world but the practical tools for navigating it. As we delve into the practical aspects of Stoicism, you'll discover how to simplify complex decisions, apply effective frameworks, and see the benefits of these practices through real-life applications.

SIMPLIFYING STOIC PRINCIPLES FOR DAILY DECISION-MAKING

Stoicism teaches us that the essence of good decision-making lies in recognizing what is within our control and what is not. This understanding is crucial because it liberates us from the frustration of trying to influence what we cannot change and directs our energy toward what we can actually affect. By distilling Stoic principles into simple, actionable advice, we can make this wisdom a substantial tool in our daily lives.

One effective way to apply Stoic wisdom is by using the Dichotomy of Control to assess situations. When faced with a decision, ask yourself: "Is this within my control?" If yes, you proceed with actions that can influence the outcome; if no, focus on your response to the situation instead. This straightforward framework can dramatically simplify the decision-making process by clearing away unnecessary concerns and concentrating your efforts on areas where you can make a real impact.

Consider a common scenario: a disagreement at a family gathering. Here, you cannot control the opinions or emotions of others, but you can control your responses and actions. A Stoic approach would be to remain calm, listen actively, and respond with respect and clarity, aiming for understanding rather than victory. This not only reduces personal stress but often leads to more productive and harmonious interactions.

Another area where Stoic principles prove invaluable is in career decisions. When contemplating a job change, for example, focus on elements such as preparing your resume, acquiring new skills, or networking—factors you can control. Worry less about the fluctuating job market or the decisions of potential employers, as these are outside your direct influence. This approach not only makes the process less daunting but also enhances your preparedness, making you a more compelling candidate when the opportunity arises.

Regular reflection is the key to reinforcing these decision-making frameworks. Engage in a nightly review where you examine the decisions you made throughout the day, assessing them through the lens of Stoic principles. This practice not only deepens your understanding of Stoicism but also embeds its wisdom into your daily routine, gradually transforming your approach to decision-making.

Reflective Exercise: Evening Review

Each evening, take a few moments to reflect on a significant decision you made that day. Write it down in a journal and evaluate it:

- What aspects of the situation were within your control?
- How did you respond to those aspects?
- What were the outcomes, and how do they align with your Stoic values? This simple exercise can provide profound insights into your decision-making process and help cultivate a more Stoic approach to daily challenges.

By embedding these simplified Stoic principles into your daily decision-making, you not only make life more manageable but also more meaningful. The clarity that comes from focusing on what you can control, paired with the ethical framework provided by Stoic qualities, equips you to handle life's complexities with confidence and composure. This chapter will continue to explore practical Stoic tools that you can incorporate into various aspects of your daily life, enhancing both your personal growth and your impact on the world around you.

THE STOIC MORNING ROUTINE: STARTING YOUR DAY WITH SERENITY

Imagine greeting each day not with a rush of anxiety or a barrage of unchecked emails but with a moment of serene contemplation. A Stoic morning ritual can provide just that—a structured start to your day that centers your thoughts and grounds your actions in

Stoic wisdom. Such a routine often involves meditation, journaling, and the reading of Stoic texts, each action woven together to cultivate a mindset of calm and clarity.

Meditation, in the Stoic sense, involves a focus on mindfulness and presence. This practice isn't just about tranquility but about preparing the mind to face the day's challenges with a focus on what you can control. You might spend a few minutes each morning in quiet reflection, considering the day ahead and reminding yourself of your capacity to meet it with composure and rationality. This daily meditation helps anchor you in the present, steering your mind away from "what ifs" and worries about the future that can so often unsettle your day before it even begins.

Journaling, too, plays a crucial role in the Stoic morning routine. This isn't simply about recording events but about reflecting on your interactions and thoughts through the lens of Stoic philosophy. What virtues were you able to practice yesterday? What could you have handled more wisely? What are today's opportunities for practicing Stoicism? These morning entries can help you set a deliberate tone for the day, one that aligns with Stoic ideals such as wisdom, justice, courage, and moderation.

Reading Stoic texts each morning, whether from Marcus Aurelius' *Meditations* or Epictetus' *Enchiridion,* serves as a daily reminder of the principles you aspire to live by. These readings provide philosophical insights that can be thought over throughout the day, serving as a guide in times of difficulty or decision. The words of these Stoic philosophers remind us of the resilience and moral fortitude we can aspire to, providing both comfort and challenge as we start our day.

This structured start is not about rigid adherence to a checklist but about creating a space for mental and emotional preparation. It's about starting the day with a ritual that reinforces your values and centers your mind, setting a tone of calm and purpose. These moments of morning serenity are not just pauses in the rush; they are investments in a more thoughtful, effective, and balanced way of living.

Throughout the day, the practice of visualization can extend the benefits of your morning routine. Before each significant event or decision, take a moment to visualize the upcoming situation. See yourself handling the scenario with composure and adhering to Stoic principles. What would wisdom look like in this meeting? How can courage show itself in this conversation? This practice not only prepares you for the day's challenges but also strengthens your ongoing engagement with Stoic ideals.

Numerous individuals have found that implementing such a morning routine significantly enhances their daily experience. Consider the testimony of a school teacher who discovered that starting the day with Stoic meditation and journaling allowed her to handle classroom challenges with much more composure and empathy. Or a business executive whose morning routine of reading and reflection led to more thoughtful leadership and decision-making. These stories underscore the practical benefits of a Stoic morning—enhanced calm, improved decision-making, and a day constantly aligned with one's deeper values.

Incorporating these practices each morning sets a foundation of tranquility and intention, providing you with the tools to navigate the day's complexities with Stoic calm and wisdom. Whether you face professional challenges, personal decisions, or unexpected difficulties, a morning grounded in Stoic practice prepares you to meet each with equanimity and resolve. This is the power of a Stoic morning: it does not change the external world, but it profoundly transforms your ability to engage with it, fostering a day lived with intention, virtue, and peace.

STOIC RESPONSES TO COMMON WORKPLACE CHALLENGES

The modern workplace can often feel like a battleground where headaches such as looming deadlines, difficult coworkers, and the ever-present fear of job insecurity conspire to disrupt our peace of mind. Stoicism, with its focus on inner tranquility and rational response, offers powerful tools to navigate these common challenges. By understanding and implementing Stoic strategies, you can transform the way you interact with your work environment, maintaining both effectiveness and calm in the face of daily workplace pressures.

One predominant source of stress in any job is the pressure of tight deadlines. The anxiety of racing against the clock can not only diminish the quality of your work but can also lead to burnout. Here, the Stoic practice of focusing on effort rather than outcome can be particularly beneficial. Instead of fixating on the deadline itself—a factor often outside your complete control—concentrate on doing the best work possible in the time available. This shift in focus aligns with the Stoic principle of accepting external events as they occur while maintaining control over your actions and attitudes. By doing so, you not only enhance your peace of mind but often your efficiency as well.

Interpersonal conflicts with coworkers also pose significant challenges in the workplace. Stoicism teaches us that other people's behaviors and opinions are outside our direct control and, thus, should not dictate our inner state. When dealing with difficult colleagues, apply the Stoic strategy of objective judgment—view these interactions as opportunities to practice patience and understanding. Before reacting, pause and consider the intentions behind their actions, which often stem from their personal challenges or insecurities. Responding with empathy and maintaining professional decorum not only diffuses potential conflicts but also fosters a more positive work atmosphere.

Job insecurity is another stressor that can cause significant anxiety, given its direct impact on our livelihood and future plans. Stoicism addresses this fear by reminding us of the transience of all external conditions and urging us to find security within ourselves. Cultivate an 'inner citadel' by developing skills and a mindset that enhances your employability and adaptability. Focus on building a robust professional network and staying updated with industry trends, making you better prepared to handle whatever career changes may come. This proactive approach not only mitigates fear but also empowers you to take charge of your career trajectory.

Assertive Communication in the Stoic Workplace

Effective communication is critical to managing workplace stress and fostering a collaborative environment. Stoicism, which promotes clarity of thought and expression, can significantly enhance your communication skills. When expressing your needs or setting boundaries, do so with clarity and respect, ensuring your message is understood but not imposed. For instance, if a project's deadline is leading to an unreasonable workload, calmly explain the situation to your manager, propose viable solutions, or request additional resources. This method of communication—not aggressive but assertively clear—ensures that your professional boundaries are respected while maintaining positive relationships with your colleagues.

The concept of the 'inner citadel' is particularly relevant when developing resilience against workplace stress. This Stoic metaphor describes a mental fortress that protects your rational and emotional core from external disturbances. Building your inner citadel involves regular self-reflection, practicing mindfulness, and adhering to your ethical values, which together fortify your psychological resilience. With a strong inner citadel, you can face workplace challenges without losing your composure, making decisions that reflect both your professional judgment and your Stoic principles.

By applying these Stoic strategies to everyday workplace challenges, you not only enhance your professional effectiveness but also contribute to a healthier, more harmonious work environment. These practices allow you to navigate the complexities of your job with a calm and focused demeanor, turning daily challenges into opportunities for personal and professional growth.

BUILDING EMOTIONAL RESILIENCE THROUGH STOIC REFLECTION

Emotional resilience, from a Stoic perspective, is defined as the capacity to endure life's challenges with a steady demeanor, adapt to changing circumstances, and recover effectively from adversity. This resilience is not a passive acceptance but an active engagement with life's difficulties, approached with a rational and balanced mindset. Stoics believe that our reactions to adversity (not the events themselves) shape our experience and character. By managing our responses with wisdom and equanimity, we cultivate a resilience that not only helps us endure but also thrive.

Reflective practices are integral to developing Stoic resilience. These practices, such as evening self-examinations or reviews of daily actions and reactions, serve as tools for introspection and self-improvement. They allow you to dissect your day, understand your emotional responses, and assess how well your actions align with Stoic principles like courage and justice. For instance, consider a day when you faced significant professional criticism. Through Stoic reflection, you would examine not just the feedback itself but your response to it. Did you meet it with defensiveness, or did you approach it with an open, constructive attitude? By regularly engaging in such reflections, you deepen your understanding of your emotional patterns and learn to guide them more consciously.

The role of adversity in Stoic practice cannot be overstated—it is considered essential for personal growth and strengthening of character. Stoics view adversity as a form of training; just as a runner gains endurance by pushing through physical discomfort, so too can we enhance our emotional resilience by facing and reflecting on life's challenges. This perspective encourages you to see obstacles not as impediments to your happiness but as opportunities to practice virtue and strengthen your spirit. It's not the hardship itself that is valuable, but the way in which you engage with it, applying Stoic Wisdom to emerge stronger and more capable.

Historical and contemporary figures provide compelling case studies of Stoic resilience in action. Consider the example of Nelson Mandela, who, during his 27 years in prison, practiced a form of Stoic resilience by maintaining rigorous self-discipline and using the time for deep reflection and planning. Despite the harsh conditions, Mandela focused on what he could control—his mind and spirit—and emerged as a pivotal leader, embodying Stoic virtues such as endurance, dignity, and forgiveness. In a modern context, consider the CEOs and leaders who navigate the volatile ups and downs of the business world. Those who employ Stoic practices tend to approach crises not just as challenges to survive but as opportunities to refine their strategies and leadership qualities. They use Stoic reflection to assess both their successes and failures, learning from each experience to guide their future actions more wisely.

These reflections and the cultivation of resilience they foster are not just about personal survival or success; they are about contributing to the world with greater strength and wisdom. As you integrate these practices into your daily life, you build not only your capacity to overcome personal challenges but also your ability to impact those around you positively. This chapter has explored how Stoic tools—simplified decision-making frameworks, morning routines focused on serenity, and strategies for handling workplace challenges—can be practically applied to foster resilience and wisdom in everyday life. As we continue, remember that each Stoic practice is a step toward not simply surviving in the world but thriving within it, armed with virtue and resilience.

In sum, this chapter underscores the transformative power of Stoic reflection in building emotional resilience. By embracing reflective practices, understanding the constructive role of adversity, and learning from both historical and contemporary examples, you are equipping yourself with the tools to navigate life's challenges with grace and strength. As we move forward, these principles will continue to guide us, proving that Stoicism is not merely a philosophy of ancient times but a vibrant, living guide for anyone seeking a more fulfilled and resilient life.

THE DICHOTOMY OF CONTROL

I n the intricate dance of life, where we constantly juggle our desires, responsibilities, and dreams against the backdrop of a world that often seems chaotic and unpredictable, how do we find our footing? The Stoic philosophy offers a profound and practical guideline known as the Dichotomy of Control. Understanding and applying this principle can not only transform how you navigate challenges but also deepen your sense of peace and empowerment. Let's explore this foundational concept of Stoicism, unravel common misconceptions, and discover how embracing what we can control—and letting go of what we cannot—can lead to a profoundly effective and fulfilling life.

UNDERSTANDING WHAT YOU CAN AND CANNOT CONTROL

At the heart of Stoic Wisdom is the recognition of a simple yet life-changing truth: some things in life are within our control, and many are not. This understanding is crucial because it directly influences our emotional and psychological landscape.

The Stoics teach us that our actions, beliefs, and responses are within our sphere of control. In contrast, external events—the actions of other people, the thoughts they harbor, and the myriad circumstances that unfold around us—lie outside this sphere.

Consider the frustration of being stuck in a traffic jam, an event that is clearly beyond your control. The stress and irritation that often accompany such situations aren't caused by the traffic but by our reaction to it. Here, Stoicism offers a liberating perspective: while you cannot control the traffic, you can control your response. Instead of succumbing to frustration, you might choose to listen to an audiobook, reflect on your day, or enjoy some rare solitude. This shift in focus—from the uncontrollable to the controllable—is the key to maintaining tranquility.

However, this principle is often misunderstood. A common misconception is the belief that with enough effort, one can control external outcomes. This misunderstanding can lead to significant frustration and exhaustion because it sets us up for failure when, inevitably, the world does not conform to our will. Stoicism teaches us to invest our energy wisely, focusing on our actions and attitudes, which are ours to command.

Highlighting the Importance of Acceptance

Another critical aspect of the Dichotomy of Control is acceptance —accepting that we cannot control everything. This acceptance is not about resignation but about recognizing reality as it is. By accepting the limits of our control, we avoid wasting energy on pointless resistance and instead devote ourselves to actions that can genuinely make a difference. This acceptance also fosters peace of mind; when we stop fighting against the uncontrollable, we can find serenity even during life's storms.

The power of this principle extends beyond individual peace to interpersonal relationships and professional environments. In the workplace, for example, you might encounter situations where colleagues make decisions that affect you yet are outside your control. Here, Stoicism advises focusing on your response: advocating calmly for your interests, preparing for various outcomes, and finding ways to adapt constructively.

The Dichotomy of Control, therefore, is not just a philosophical statement but a practical strategy for living more effectively. It teaches us to navigate life not by attempting to control the uncontrollable but by mastering what is genuinely ours: our actions, our responses, and our decisions. This mastery leads to a more empowered and effective life, marked not by a lack of challenges but by our skillful and serene navigation through them.

PRACTICAL EXERCISES TO ENHANCE AWARENESS OF CONTROL

Incorporating Stoic principles into your daily life can significantly enhance your ability to distinguish between what you can and cannot control, fostering a more profound sense of peace and effectiveness. To cultivate this awareness, I recommend integrating specific, straightforward exercises into your routine. These practices, designed to sharpen your recognition of control, help you to focus your energies more wisely and respond to life's unpredictabilities with composure and insight.

One such practice is daily journaling, a method that not only aids in reflection but also the practical application of Stoic principles. Each evening, dedicate a few minutes to jot down the day's events, categorizing them under 'controllable' and 'uncontrollable.' For instance, you might note a heated discussion with a colleague under 'uncontrollable,' as their reactions are not within your power. Conversely, your choice to remain calm or to engage respectfully can be noted under 'controllable'. This simple act of categorization helps to internalize the dichotomy of control, gradually shifting your focus from external circumstances to your internal responses. Over time, this practice can transform your approach to challenges, leading you to a more proactive and centered engagement with life.

Mindfulness practices also play a crucial role in enhancing awareness of control. Mindfulness involves maintaining a moment-by-moment awareness of our thoughts, feelings, bodily sensations, and surrounding environment. By cultivating mindfulness, you develop the ability to observe your reactions to situations without immediately acting on them. This pause is crucial; it provides the space to assess whether you are trying to control the uncontrollable. Regular mindfulness meditation can be particularly effective. Dedicate a few minutes each day to sit quietly and focus on your breath. When thoughts or worries arise, gently acknowledge them and assess whether they concern things within your control. If not, visualize setting them aside, focusing instead on your breathing and the present moment. This practice not only reduces stress but also reinforces the Stoic discipline of focusing on the present and what you can influence.

Developing a 'Control Checklist'

To further this awareness, I suggest creating a 'control checklist,' a simple yet powerful tool to use in real-time situations. This checklist should include questions like: "Can I control this situation?", "What aspects can I influence?" and "Am I focusing on my reaction or trying to control the outcome?" Keep this checklist accessible—perhaps on a small card in your wallet or as a note on your phone. In moments of stress or decision, run through this checklist to realign your focus toward what you can effectively manage. This practice not only saves you from unnecessary frustration but also enhances your decision-making and problem-solving abilities by keeping your energy directed toward actionable areas.

Using Scenarios for Practice

To solidify your understanding and application of the dichotomy of control, consider setting aside time each week to analyze and discuss specific scenarios, either on your own or with a group. For example, imagine you are planning a special family event, and the weather forecast suddenly predicts rain. Explore how you might apply the dichotomy of control here. You cannot control the weather, but you can control your preparations, such as arranging for indoor alternatives or providing umbrellas for guests. By discussing and dissecting such scenarios, you can refine your ability to distinguish between controllable and uncontrollable elements, enhancing your adaptability and resourcefulness in real-life situations.

Through these exercises—journaling, mindfulness, the control checklist, and scenario analysis—you equip yourself with practical tools to embody Stoic Wisdom in your daily life. These practices not only deepen your philosophical understanding but also enhance your practical skills in managing life's uncertainties with grace and effectiveness. In doing so, you cultivate a life not just of survival but of success, characterized by an empowered serenity and a proactive engagement with the world.

LETTING GO OF ANXIETY OVER THE UNCONTROLLABLE

In our quest for control over our lives, we often find ourselves ensnared by anxiety—an emotional response that not only disrupts our harmony but can significantly hinder our ability to enjoy life and perform effectively. This anxiety frequently stems from a deep-seated desire to control what is fundamentally uncontrollable. Understanding this relationship between control and anxiety is the first step toward alleviating the latter, and Stoicism provides a valuable framework for this understanding.

Anxiety often arises when we face situations that remind us of our limitations—events or outcomes that we cannot predict or control, such as the health of a loved one, the stability of our job, or the state of global affairs. The Stoic approach teaches us that this anxiety is not a direct result of the situations themselves but from our perceptions and the unrealistic expectation that we should be able to control these external factors. Recognizing that some aspects of life are simply beyond our control can significantly reduce the anxiety associated with them. This recognition frees us from the burden of trying to control the uncontrollable and directs our efforts towards areas where we can actually make a difference—in our attitudes and responses.

Cognitive reframing techniques can be particularly effective in aiding in this transformation of perspective. These techniques involve altering your mental approach to a situation and changing your emotional response in the process. For instance, instead of viewing a looming project deadline as a stress-inducing demand, reframe it as an opportunity to showcase your skills and dedication. Similarly, if worrying about a family member's health, reframe your concern into proactive engagement—such as encouraging healthier lifestyle choices or supporting medical appointments. By reframing these situations, you shift from a passive state of worry about uncontrollable outcomes to an active state of engagement with controllable actions, thereby reducing anxiety and increasing effectiveness.

Another powerful practice to lower anxiety is to establish a routine of relinquishment—a dedicated time to consciously let go of the things outside your control. This could be a daily or weekly session where you reflect on the events or worries occupying your mind and categorically release those that you cannot influence. For example, you might write down your concerns and physically mark those that are beyond your control, symbolically setting them aside. Documenting the emotional impact of this practice can be enlightening; many find that this routine not only clarifies what is within their control but also brings a profound sense of relief and lightness as the burden of unnecessary worries is lifted.

The effectiveness of these strategies is not just theoretical but is supported by numerous success stories. Take the case of a corporate lawyer who struggled with chronic anxiety about case outcomes, client reactions, and courtroom performances—factors that were often unpredictable and beyond her direct control. By applying Stoic principles and engaging in cognitive reframing and routine relinquishment, she learned to focus on her preparation and effort—the aspects she could control. Over time, not only did her anxiety diminish, but her performance improved, as she was able to devote more energy to her legal strategies and client consultations rather than wasting it on unproductive worry.

In another example, a school principal used Stoicism to manage his anxiety over educational policy changes—a largely uncontrollable aspect of his job. Through regular reframing exercises, he began to see these changes not as threats but as challenges to his ability to adapt and innovate. His routine of relinquishment involved writing down his fears about policy impacts and formally setting aside time to consider practical responses rather than dwelling on potential negatives. This approach not only reduced his stress but also made him a more proactive and respected leader in his educational community.

These stories highlight a fundamental truth in Stoic philosophy: often, the control we seek is not over external events but over our own internal states. By focusing on what we can control—our responses, our mindset, our actions—we can significantly reduce our anxiety and navigate life with greater calm and confidence. This Stoic practice of focusing on the controllable, reframing our perceptions, and consciously letting go of the rest can transform not only how we handle challenges but also how we live our lives —more engaged with the present, more at peace with the uncontrollable, and more empowered in our daily actions.

HOW EMBRACING LACK OF CONTROL CAN LEAD TO GREATER HAPPINESS

In the maze of life's challenges, the act of surrendering control over external events can seem counterintuitive. Yet, it is within this paradox of surrender that a profound transformation can occur, leading to a greater sense of personal power and happiness. Stoicism teaches us that by releasing our tight grip on the illusion of control, we open ourselves to a more harmonious and joyful experience of life. Embracing what we cannot control does not diminish our power; instead, it redirects our energies towards what truly matters—our responses, our values, and our growth.

This surrender is not about giving up action but about redefining where we place our efforts and trust. It involves a deep faith in the process of life, believing that even in chaos, there is a pattern that will emerge, a lesson to be learned, and growth to be experienced.

Trusting this process means having faith in our own capabilities to adapt and find meaning, regardless of circumstances. This faith is crucial, for it is what allows us to face uncertainty with courage rather than fear. It anchors us in the belief that whatever the outcome, we have the resilience and the wisdom to navigate through it.

Consider the natural world, which thrives on a balance of control and surrender. A tree does not try to control the wind, the rain, or the sun; it simply grows, adapts, and thrives in the midst of these uncontrollable forces. Similarly, when we embrace the uncontrollable aspects of our lives with grace, we tap into a more profound source of happiness and peace. Engaging with community and nature serves as a powerful reminder of this balance. By being part of a community, whether participating in local events, volunteering, or simply connecting with neighbors, we reinforce the notion that we are part of something larger than ourselves. This involvement can alleviate the pressure of feeling that everything is up to us, offering comfort and support through collective endeavors.

Historical and philosophical anecdotes abound with figures who have embraced the limits of their control and found profound happiness. The philosopher Socrates, for instance, exhibited remarkable tranquility and humor in the face of his unjust execution, a fate he did not control and could not avoid. His acceptance of his fate, rooted in a life spent pursuing virtue and wisdom, turned his final moments into a lasting testament to the power of inner freedom. Similarly, the modern example of Viktor Frankl, who survived the horrors of a concentration camp, shows us that even in extreme conditions, our attitudes and responses hold the key to our freedom and happiness. Frankl's philosophy, that one could find meaning and personal growth in every moment of existence, no matter how brutal, provides a modern-day echo of Stoic resilience and joy in the face of life's uncontrollability.

As you reflect on these ideas, consider how you might start to relinquish the need for control in your life. Perhaps it begins with a simple daily affirmation, acknowledging what you can and cannot control, or maybe it involves a more active engagement with the community or nature. Whatever form it takes, the practice of embracing the uncontrollable not only enhances your well-being but also enriches your interactions with the world around you. By surrendering control where it cannot be actually exerted, you gain a better command over your own life, navigating your experiences with an empowered serenity and a joyful heart.

In the journey through the pages of this book, we have explored not only the theoretical underpinnings of Stoicism but also its practical applications, from understanding the dichotomy of control to embracing the paradox of surrender. These principles, woven into the fabric of daily life, offer a robust framework for dealing with the complexities of modern existence. As we move forward, remember that the essence of Stoic Wisdom lies not merely in enduring life's challenges but in transforming them into avenues for personal growth and fulfillment.

In the next chapter, we will delve deeper into the Stoic practices that can help you cultivate resilience and inner peace, ensuring that you are not just surviving but thriving, no matter what life throws your way. This journey of exploration and application continues to unfold, offering ever more profound insights into how Stoicism can illuminate and enrich your life path.

RELATIONSHIPS THROUGH A STOIC LENS

Navigating the intricate webs of relationships, be it with friends, family, or colleagues, can often feel like trying to sail in turbulent waters. Conflicts arise, and under the force of emotional winds, our reactions might steer us away from the tranquil harbors we aim for. But what if you could equip yourself with the philosophical compass of Stoicism, guiding you to navigate these interactions with poise and understanding? Stoicism, with its profound insights into human behavior and emotion, provides invaluable tools for managing relationships in a way that not only preserves but enriches them.

THE STOIC'S GUIDE TO HANDLING CONFLICT IN RELATIONSHIPS

Conflicts in relationships often spring from misaligned perceptions. Each person views the world through their own lens, colored by individual experiences, emotions, and expectations. Stoicism teaches us that these differing perceptions are a fundamental aspect of human nature and that recognizing this can significantly de-escalate potential tensions. When you acknowl-edge that another's viewpoint is merely their perception of reality, not an objective truth, you open the door to understanding and reconciliation rather than conflict.

To cultivate this understanding, Stoicism encourages the practice of empathy and perspective-taking. Imagine stepping into the shoes of another, seeing through their eyes, and feeling with their heart. This exercise does not just broaden your understanding of their actions and reactions; it fosters a deeper connection, a vital element in building and sustaining harmonious relationships. For instance, if a friend reacts angrily to a canceled plan, instead of mirroring their frustration, try to understand the underlying feel-ings. Perhaps they had been looking forward to this as a much-needed break in a stressful week. Recognizing this can shift your response from one of irritation to one of compassion, paving the way for a calm and constructive conversation.

Implementing Stoic calm in heated moments is another powerful strategy. Stoicism doesn't teach suppression of emotion but rather the management of it. One effective technique is the pause—a deliberate cessation of immediate reaction. When a conflict arises, instead of responding in the heat of the moment, take a deep breath or even step away if necessary. This pause gives you the space to collect your thoughts, temper your emotions, and approach the situation with a level head. By responding rather than reacting, you embody the Stoic ideal of self-control, turning potential arguments into opportunities for open and productive dialogues.

Moreover, Stoicism provides Wisdom in choosing your battles wisely. Not every disagreement demands your energy, and not every conflict merits confrontation. Some issues, when viewed through the lens of Stoic discernment, reveal themselves to be minor or based on quickly resolved misunderstandings. Stoicism teaches us to focus on what truly matters—such as respect, understanding, and love. Before engaging in or escalating a conflict, ask yourself whether this issue will matter in the long run or if it's merely a distraction from the health and happiness of your relationship. Often, you'll find that letting go of minor grievances can lead to greater peace and stability in your relationships.

Exercise: Reflective Journaling on Relationship Conflicts

Consider keeping a reflective journal where you document and analyze conflicts that arise in your relationships. For each conflict, write down:

- The perceived cause of the conflict.
- Your initial emotional response.
- How you chose to handle the situation.
- The outcome of the conflict.
- Lessons learned and how you might handle a similar situation in the future.

This practice not only aids in self-reflection but also helps in developing a more Stoic approach to handling relationship conflicts, focusing on understanding, empathy, and the essential virtues that strengthen bonds.

By embracing these Stoic practices, you equip yourself with the tools to handle conflicts not just with effectiveness but with a grace that enriches your connections with others. These strategies, grounded in ancient wisdom, are profoundly relevant in our modern lives, helping to transform potential discord into opportunities for deeper understanding and stronger relationships. As you continue to apply these teachings, you may find that the Stoic approach not only resolves conflicts but also prevents them, fostering an atmosphere of mutual respect and peace in all your interpersonal engagements.

LOVE AND STOICISM: MAINTAINING INDIVIDUALITY AND HARMONY

In the delicate dance of relationships, especially those tinged with romance, the balance between emotional investment and maintaining rational independence is often a tightrope walk. Stoicism provides insightful guidance on navigating this balance with its deep roots in understanding the nature of emotions and human interactions. The Stoic practice of caring deeply for others while sustaining an inner detachment is not about emotional coldness, but rather about protecting one's peace of mind. This approach helps maintain clarity and composure, allowing you to love freely without becoming overly dependent on the reciprocation or behavior of your partner.

This detachment is crucial in preserving your well-being in relationships. It involves seeing and appreciating your partner for who they are but also recognizing that your emotional state does not need to be entirely contingent upon their actions or moods. For instance, if a partner is going through a rough patch and becomes distant, a Stoic approach would be to offer support without feeling personally slighted or overly distressed. This balanced attitude helps you remain supportive and present yet emotionally stable, whether the relationship is flourishing or facing challenges.

Cultivating self-sufficiency in relationships is another cornerstone of Stoic practice. It encourages you to find sources of happiness and fulfillment from within yourself rather than relying solely on your partner or friends. This self-sufficiency is about developing your hobbies, interests, and emotional resilience. Engaging in activities that fulfill you independently of your relationship not only reduces the pressure on your partner to be your sole source of happiness but also leads to a healthier, more balanced relationship. For example, pursuing a personal hobby or career ambition can provide a sense of accomplishment and satisfaction that complements the joys found in your relationship rather than competing with it.

Harmonizing personal growth with relational growth is an essential aspect of Stoic love. Stoicism teaches that personal virtues such as wisdom, courage, and temperance can greatly enhance relationships. Conversely, healthy relationships can foster personal growth, creating a virtuous cycle. This mutual support is about encouraging each other to pursue individual goals and qualities, not in a spirit of competition but in one of collaboration. For instance, practicing temperance might help you manage emotional reactions within your relationship, while your relationship might provide opportunities to practice and reinforce this feature through real-life challenges and interactions.

This synergy between personal and relational growth is encapsulated beautifully in the Stoic idea that love should be based on the admiration of each other's qualities. Stoic love is not merely an emotional affection but a profound connection that inspires both parties to strive towards a life of mutual benefit. In a Stoic relationship, partners motivate each other to be their best selves, not through criticism or control but through example and mutual support. This type of relationship is deeply fulfilling because it is based not just on emotional attachment but on a shared commitment to living virtuously.

By integrating these Stoic principles into your relationships, you cultivate not only a deeper connection with your partner but also a more profound understanding and application of Stoicism in your life. This approach to relationships offers a pathway to true companionship, where love is expressed not just in words or emotions but through a shared journey towards virtue and fulfillment. Through this lens, every interaction in your relationship becomes an opportunity to practice and reinforce Stoic principles, enriching both your life and that of your partner.

EFFECTIVE COMMUNICATION STRATEGIES INSPIRED BY STOICISM

In the realm of human interactions, the art of communication is paramount. Stoicism, with its profound emphasis on integrity and rationality, provides a robust framework for enhancing how we express ourselves and connect with others. Promoting transparent and honest communication is foundational in Stoic practice, reflecting the virtue of integrity. When you engage in conversations, whether they are casual chats or significant discussions, being honest and sincere not only fosters trust but also builds a solid foundation for meaningful relationships. This transparency means being open about your thoughts and feelings but also being candid about your limitations and uncertainties. For instance, in a professional setting, rather than agreeing to a deadline you know is unrealistic, a Stoic approach would be to express your concerns honestly and negotiate a more feasible timeline, which not only ensures you can deliver quality work but also establishes your reliability and respect for truth.

Moreover, Stoicism teaches the importance of listening—a skill that is often overshadowed by the urge to speak and be heard. Authentic listening, from a Stoic perspective, isn't just about hearing the words that others say but involves a deeper level of engagement. It's about tuning into the emotions and intentions behind those words. This form of empathetic listening can transform interactions, making the person you're communicating with genuinely feel understood and valued. It involves an active effort to see the world from the other person's perspective, which not only enriches your understanding but can also diffuse potential conflicts before they escalate. For example, if a friend seems upset over a seemingly trivial matter, carefully listening might reveal underlying issues such as stress or insecurity that are the true roots of their distress. By responding to these deeper issues rather than the surface symptoms, you can provide support that is genuinely effective and appreciated.

The realm of non-verbal communication also holds substantial weight in Stoic practice. Stoics understand that much of what we communicate is not transmitted through words but through our body language, facial expressions, and even our silence. Being mindful of non-verbal cues can provide critical insights into others' thoughts and feelings, often revealing more than their words might convey. For instance, a colleague might say they agree with a decision, but their crossed arms and averted gaze might suggest otherwise. Observing these signs enables you to address concerns that haven't been explicitly stated, fostering an atmosphere of openness and trust. Furthermore, being conscious of your own non-verbal signals can help you communicate more effectively. A calm demeanor and open posture can convey confidence and receptivity, encouraging others to engage more openly with you.

Lastly, Stoicism advocates for a balanced expression of assertiveness and kindness—a combination that is particularly powerful in communication. Being assertive means expressing your needs and boundaries clearly and confidently, without passivity or aggression. This assertiveness, tempered with kindness, aligns with Stoic principles of courage and justice, ensuring that your communications not only respect your values but also consider the well-being of others. For example, if you feel overwhelmed by your workload, expressing this to your supervisor assertively yet respectfully can lead to a more manageable allocation of tasks. Similarly, if a friend repeatedly cancels plans at the last minute, addressing the issue directly yet kindly can lead to a discussion about respect and reliability in your relationship.

These strategies—promoting honesty, practicing empathetic listening, observing non-verbal cues, and combining assertiveness with kindness—are not just techniques but reflections of deeper Stoic values. They are about respecting yourself and others, striving for harmony and understanding, and navigating complex human relationships with wisdom and grace. As you continue to integrate these Stoic principles into your communication practices, you will likely find that not only do your interactions become more effective and satisfying, but they also become more enriching, reflecting the profound Stoic pursuit of living a virtuous and meaningful life.

FORGIVENESS AND LETTING GO: A STOIC APPROACH

Forgiveness in the realm of Stoicism is not merely about absolving others but is more profoundly about restoring one's peace of mind —seen as a release of resentment and a pathway back to emotional equilibrium. The Stoics believed that harboring resentment ties us to the past, a realm over which we have no control and which distracts us from the present moment where our power truly lies. Forgiveness, therefore, is fundamentally about reclaiming control over our emotional well-being by letting go of grievances that cloud our tranquility.

This process begins with understanding the inherent flaws and frailties that are part of being human. Recognizing that everyone, including ourselves, is capable of making mistakes or acting out of ignorance, fear, or distress can change the emotional landscape from one of anger to one of empathy. This shift is crucial because it allows us to see the situation from a broader perspective where our personal hurt does not obscure our capacity for compassion. For instance, if a colleague's harsh words during a stressful project upset you, understanding their pressure and anxiety can help mitigate your hurt feelings and lead you toward forgiveness.

Practically, forgiveness involves a series of intentional steps. The first step is to clearly acknowledge the hurt or damage done rather than denying or diminishing it. This acknowledgment is vital as it validates your feelings and defines what exactly needs to be forgiven. Following this, engage in a deliberate decision-making process where you choose to let go of the resentment. This might involve writing a letter of forgiveness (which you do not necessarily have to send) or simply saying out loud to yourself that you choose to forgive. The act of deciding to forgive is empowering—it shifts the situation from something that happens to you to something you control.

Next, actively work on releasing the emotional charge connected to the memory of the offense. This could be through meditation, where you visualize letting go of the resentment, or through physical activity like running or yoga, where you imagine releasing the negative feelings with each breath or movement. Over time, these practices can diminish the emotional weight of past grievances, helping to restore your inner peace.

The benefits of practicing forgiveness are profound and complex. On a personal level, letting go of grudges can lead to decreased anxiety, lower blood pressure, and overall improved mental health. These changes occur because forgiveness reduces the physiological burden that anger and resentment place on the body. Emotionally, forgiving others can lead to heightened feelings of happiness and contentment as you reclaim the energy previously consumed by negative emotions. Relationally, forgiveness can transform dynamics, paving the way for healthier and more understanding interactions. It removes the barriers of bitterness and allows for the possibility of rebuilding trust and empathy, essential components for robust relationships.

In Stoicism, the act of forgiveness is not just an occasional remedy for grievances but a regular practice that maintains and restores peace. It aligns perfectly with the Stoic endeavor to live a virtuous life, for it requires and nurtures virtues like courage, justice, temperance, and wisdom. Each act of forgiveness is both a practice of these virtues and a step towards a more profound, more peaceful, and more resilient life.

As we culminate this exploration of relationships through a Stoic lens, we've traversed the terrain of conflict management, the balancing act in love, effective communication, and the freeing act of forgiveness. Each of these facets, enriched by Stoic Wisdom, invites you to engage more deeply, more serenely, and more meaningfully in your relationships. The next chapter will delve into managing emotions and personal growth, continuing to build on the solid foundation of Stoic practices we've established thus far. Here, we will explore how Stoicism not only helps in navigating external challenges but also profoundly transforms our internal landscape.

MANAGING EMOTIONS AND GROWTH

I n the rich tapestry of human experience, emotions weave vibrant, often tumultuous patterns, influencing everything from our daily interactions to our most profound life decisions. This chapter delves into the Stoic approach to managing emotions, particularly focusing on anger and frustration—emotions that, if left unchecked, can disrupt our peace and hinder our growth. Here, you'll learn not only to understand these powerful feelings but also to manage them with wisdom and grace, using Stoic practices that have stood the test of time.

STOIC PRACTICES TO CURB ANGER AND FRUSTRATION

Understanding the Triggers and Responses

Anger, often seen as a destructive force, can actually serve as a signal, pointing us toward unresolved issues or unmet expectations. The first step in managing anger is to recognize what triggers it. These triggers can be as varied as feeling undervalued at work, facing disrespect in a relationship, or dealing with the chronic stress of daily commutes. Once recognized, it's crucial to observe how this anger manifests in your thoughts and behaviors —do you withdraw silently or lash out verbally? Understanding these patterns is critical to addressing the root causes and reshaping your responses.

Implementing the Stoic Pause and Reflect Technique

The Stoic pause is a powerful tool in your emotional arsenal. When you feel anger rising, give yourself the gift of time—just a few seconds can transform your reaction. During this pause, engage in reflective questioning: "What is truly causing my anger? Is my response going to be beneficial or detrimental? What would a wise person do in my position?" This moment of introspection can shift your perspective from a knee-jerk reaction to a considered response, allowing you to address the issue with composure and clarity.

Applying the Principle of Impermanence

Stoicism teaches us that all external events are transient—they come and go. By internalizing this principle of impermanence, you can lessen the intensity of your anger. For instance, if you are infuriated by a project setback, remind yourself that this situation is temporary and will soon be just a memory. This broader perspective reduces the emotional weight of the event, helping you approach it with a balanced mindset and focus on constructive solutions rather than getting bogged down by frustration.

Encouraging the Adoption of Empathy

Expanding your perspective to include the intentions and circumstances of others can significantly reduce feelings of anger and lead to more compassionate responses. When someone acts in a way that triggers your anger, try to understand their motives and background. Perhaps they are under stress or unaware of the impact of their actions. By practicing empathy, you not only mitigate your anger but also open up pathways for more transparent communication and more effective conflict resolution.

Interactive Element: Reflective Journaling Exercise

To integrate these Stoic practices into your daily life, maintain a reflective journal. Each night, jot down instances where you felt anger or frustration during the day. Describe the trigger, your initial reaction, and how you applied Stoic techniques to handle the situation. Reflect on what worked and what could be improved. This exercise not only solidifies your learning but also tracks your progress over time, enhancing your ability to manage these challenging emotions with increasing skill and wisdom.

Through these Stoic practices—understanding triggers, pausing to reflect, recognizing impermanence, and practicing empathy—you can transform your approach to anger and frustration. Instead of being overwhelmed by these emotions, you learn to handle them with grace and effectiveness, using them as tools for personal growth and better relationships. As we continue to explore the vast landscape of handling emotions through Stoicism, remember that each step you take is not just about controlling feelings but about cultivating a deeper, more resilient version of yourself, ready to face the world with confidence and composure.

TURNING ENVY AND JEALOUSY INTO MOTIVATORS WITH STOICISM

Envy and jealousy, if left unchecked, can erode our inner peace and cloud our perceptions of our own lives. Yet, viewed through the lens of Stoicism, these emotions can serve as valuable tools for self-reflection and personal growth. Rather than allowing these feelings to foster resentment, you can transform them into catalysts for enhancing your own life and achieving genuine fulfillment. This transformative approach involves redefining success, utilizing envy as a reflective tool, cultivating an abundance mindset, and turning jealousy into a motivational force.

Redefining Personal Success

In our society, success is often measured by external benchmarks: career achievements, material acquisitions, or social status. However, Stoicism invites you to redefine success based on internal virtues and personal excellence. This internal measure focuses not on comparing yourself to others but on assessing your growth and integrity. Ask yourself: "Am I more patient, kind, and wise than I was last year?" By shifting the focus from external validation to internal development, you not only foster self-contentment but also insulate yourself from the destabilizing effects of envy. When you know your worth and your goals are aligned with your deepest values, the achievements of others become less a source of jealousy and more a reminder of the many paths to personal excellence.

Using Envy as a Mirror

When feelings of envy arise, instead of pushing them away or letting them sour your mood, use them as mirrors to reflect on your desires and aspirations. What is it about someone else's situation that triggers your envy? Is it their professional success, their relationships, or perhaps their lifestyle? These reflections can reveal essential truths about what you value and what might be missing or unfulfilled in your own life. Instead of resenting others' successes, analyze these feelings to understand better what changes you might pursue in your own life to achieve fulfillment. This introspective process not only diminishes envy but also clarifies your goals, steering you toward a more authentic and satisfying life path.

Developing a Mindset of Abundance

One of the most effective antidotes to envy and jealousy is cultivating an abundance mindset. This perspective focuses on appreciating what you already have rather than fixating on what others possess. Begin by regularly counting your blessings—acknowledge your talents, cherish your relationships, and celebrate your progress, no matter how small. Practicing gratitude shifts your focus from scarcity to abundance, reducing feelings of envy and increasing life satisfaction. When you view life as plentiful and opportunities as abundant, the success of others ceases to be a threat and instead becomes a source of inspiration.

Transforming Envy into Motivation

Finally, transform feelings of envy and jealousy into motivation to improve yourself. If a colleague's promotion sparks envy, let it motivate you to develop your skills or to take on new projects. If a friend's fitness achievements stir jealousy, use that as inspiration to prioritize your own health and wellness goals. By channeling your emotional energy positively, you not only overcome detrimental feelings but also propel yourself toward personal growth and success. This proactive approach not only enhances your well-being but also turns potentially negative emotions into stepping stones for self-improvement.

Through these practices, you can transform envy and jealousy from sources of distress into instruments of personal empowerment. By redefining success, using envy as a mirror for reflection, cultivating an abundance mindset, and converting jealousy into motivation, you align more closely with Stoic principles, leading a life driven not by comparison and resentment but by self-improvement and contentment. As you continue to apply these strategies, remember that the path to personal excellence is not about surpassing others but about surpassing your previous self, achieving a state of fulfillment that is both deeply personal and profoundly rewarding.

OVERCOMING FEAR WITH COURAGE AND RATIONAL THOUGHT

Fear, a primal human emotion, serves both as a protector and a barrier. While it can preserve us from real dangers, it often also stands as an obstacle to personal growth and fulfillment. Stoicism, with its emphasis on rationality and self-control, provides valuable tools for dissecting and managing fears, transforming them from ambiguous shadows that haunt our minds into clear challenges that we can confront and overcome. This section aims to guide you through understanding your fears, strengthening your rational thinking, cultivating authentic Stoic courage, and adopting practices such as controlled exposure to face and conquer your anxieties effectively.

Identifying Irrational Fears

First, let's differentiate between rational and irrational fears. Rational fears are those that have a factual basis in danger; for instance, the fear of touching a hot stove, which protects us from burns. Irrational fears, however, do not have a direct correlation to imminent danger. These might include fears of public speaking, heights, or even initiating personal relationships. The Stoic approach encourages us to challenge our fears by examining their validity. Ask yourself: "What is the evidence for this fear? Is there a real threat to my well-being, or is it a perceived danger?" By scrutinizing your fears under the light of reason, you can often reveal that many anxieties are not supported by reality and are instead constructs of our minds.

Strengthening Rational Thinking

Stoicism teaches us to strengthen our rational thinking to combat irrational fears, which involves systematically evaluating the worst-case scenarios of feared situations and then realistically assessing the probability of these outcomes. For example, if you're afraid of failing an important exam, consider the actual consequences: you might need to retake the test or review the material more thoroughly. When viewed rationally, the ultimate consequences are often not as catastrophic as our fears would lead us to believe. This methodical evaluation helps to minimize the perceived impact of the fear, making it more manageable and less intimidating.

Cultivating Stoic Courage

Stoic courage is not merely the absence of fear but the resolve to act rightly and virtuously despite fear's presence. It involves recognizing that genuine harm comes not from external circumstances but from failing to live according to our values. To cultivate Stoic courage, start by affirming your commitment to act with integrity, regardless of personal fears. When faced with a situation that triggers fear, remind yourself of your core values and the importance of upholding them. This focus shifts your perspective from avoiding fear to acting meaningfully despite it, empowering you to take action aligned with your principles.

Practice Exposure Therapy

One practical method to manage fear is through controlled exposure, a technique aligned with Stoic confrontational practices. This approach involves gradually and repeatedly exposing yourself to the object of your fear in a controlled, safe manner. If you're afraid of public speaking, for instance, you might start by speaking to a small, supportive group and gradually increase the audience size as your confidence grows. Over time, this repeated exposure reduces the emotional response associated with the fear, desensitizing you to the anxiety it used to provoke. This practice not only lessens the fear itself but also builds your confidence and proficiency in the previously feared activity.

By applying these Stoic strategies—identifying irrational fears, strengthening rational thinking, cultivating courage, and practicing controlled exposure—you can transform your approach to fear from one of avoidance to one of engagement. These methods encourage not merely the management of fear but its mastery, enabling you to live more freely and fully, unencumbered by irrational anxieties. As you continue to implement these practices, you may find that the fears which once seemed insurmountable become sources of strength and growth, each conquered fear adding to your resilience and zest for life.

THE ROLE OF REFLECTION IN PERSONAL STOIC GROWTH

Reflection is a cornerstone of Stoic practice, serving not just as a method for self-improvement but as a daily ritual that aligns your life more closely with the core virtues of Stoicism—wisdom, justice, courage, and temperance. By integrating the practice of daily reflection, you engage in a thoughtful examination of your thoughts, decisions, and actions, which illuminates patterns in your behavior that may be invisible during the rush of daily activities. This process allows you to pause and consider not only what you did and why you did it but also how you can improve and align your actions more closely with Stoic principles.

Imagine ending each day by sitting quietly and reviewing the events and interactions of your day. Consider the moments when you felt proud of your actions, but also those when you fell short of your Stoic ideals. Perhaps you reacted hastily to a comment from a coworker, or maybe you missed an opportunity to help a friend in need. Reflecting on these moments encourages a deeper understanding of your personal values and how effectively you are embodying them. This practice isn't about self-criticism but about self-awareness and growth—it helps you recognize your strengths and identify areas where you can develop greater virtue and resilience.

In addition to daily reflection, starting a reflective writing practice can significantly enhance your journey of personal growth. Keeping a Stoic journal allows you to record not just the events of each day but also your emotional and intellectual responses to those events. This kind of writing provides a space to explore your thoughts and feelings more deeply, to question your assumptions, and to plan how you might better handle similar situations in the future. For instance, if you find that certain events consistently trigger negative emotions, writing about them can help you understand and eventually master them. Over time, this journal becomes not just a record of your life but a roadmap of your personal evolution, showing you how far you have come and where you still wish to go.

Reflection also plays a crucial role in helping you detach emotionally from intense situations and is key to maintaining clarity and making wise decisions. Stoicism teaches that we should strive to respond to events with rationality rather than emotion. By reflecting on our experiences, particularly those that elicit strong emotional reactions, we can begin to see these situations more objectively. This detachment doesn't mean ignoring your emotions but rather understanding them as natural responses that do not have to dictate your actions. For example, if you're upset by a family member's criticism, reflection can help you understand why the criticism hurt and how you can address the underlying issues without damaging the relationship.

The benefits of reflective growth are profound. Regular reflection fosters a greater self-awareness, which is the first step toward self-mastery. It also promotes emotional regulation, helping you maintain your equanimity in challenging situations. Perhaps most importantly, reflection leads to greater wisdom and contentment. By regularly assessing and adjusting your behavior to align with Stoic virtues, you not only become a better person but also find greater satisfaction in your daily life. This satisfaction comes not from external achievements but from knowing that you are living true to your values and continuously striving to improve.

As you incorporate these reflective practices into your life, you will likely find that they not only enhance your personal growth but also enrich your relationships with others. They inspire you to be more mindful and present, both with yourself and with those around you, fostering deeper connections and a more compassionate approach to interpersonal interactions.

In this chapter, we have explored various dimensions of managing emotions and fostering personal growth through Stoicism. From understanding and curbing anger to transforming envy and overcoming fear, each section has provided practical strategies for harnessing your emotions and aligning your actions with Stoic principles. As we move forward, remember that these practices are not just exercises in self-control but pathways to a richer, more meaningful life.

STOICISM IN TIMES OF CRISIS

In life, we are invariably confronted by moments that wrench our hearts and twist our paths in unexpected ways. Loss, an inescapable human experience, comes to us all, clothed in various forms—be it the profound grief of losing a loved one, the emptiness following the end of a significant relationship, or the shock and uncertainty stemming from sudden unemployment. How does one find the strength to move forward when weighed down by such profound loss? Here, the ancient wisdom of Stoicism stands as a beacon, offering not only comfort but a powerful framework for transforming our response to loss.

FINDING STRENGTH IN STOIC PHILOSOPHY DURING LOSS

Acknowledging the Impact of Loss

The first step in navigating through loss is acknowledging its impact on our lives. It is a profound, often devastating experience that can disrupt our emotional balance and sense of stability. The pain of loss is real and intense, and Stoicism doesn't ask us to suppress this pain but to face it with courage and clarity. It teaches us that grief, though painful, is a natural response to loss, and accepting this emotion is crucial for healing.

Stoic Views on Attachment and Impermanence

Stoicism offers a unique perspective on attachment and the nature of external things. It teaches that everything around us, including our relationships and careers, is impermanent and subject to change. This might sound disheartening at first, but this recognition is vital for building internal resilience. The Stoic philosophers, such as Marcus Aurelius, remind us that our distress often arises not merely from loss itself but from our mistaken belief that we could possess something—be it a person, position, or phase of life—forever. Understanding and accepting the impermanence of all things can lessen the pain of loss, as it aligns our expectations with the reality of our transient existence.

Encouraging the Use of Stoic Reflections

In the wake of loss, Stoicism encourages the practice of reflection —turning inward to draw strength from the values and experiences we shared with what we have lost. Instead of focusing solely on the void left by the loss, Stoicism teaches us to cherish the memories and lessons learned from the relationship or situation. Reflect on what the lost loved one or job brought into your life— strength, love, growth, or resilience. These reflections are not about holding on to the past but about honoring the impact of these experiences on our personal development.

Promote the Adoption of a Forward-Looking Perspective

Stoicism is inherently forward-looking, emphasizing growth and the potential for personal development even in the face of adversity. It inspires us to shift our focus from what we have lost to the possibilities that lie ahead. This does not mean we forget the past or the pain; instead, we use it as a foundation for building a future enriched by the wisdom gained through our experiences of love and loss. Stoic optimism is not about expecting life to be easy but about recognizing our capacity to endure and grow from our challenges. It propels us to move forward, not despite our losses, but with a deeper appreciation of life's fragility and our strengths.

Reflective Exercise: Envisioning a Path Forward

Consider setting aside some time for a reflective exercise. Visualize your life as a journey with many paths. Some you have already traveled, filled with memories and lessons, while others lie ahead, unexplored and ripe with potential. Reflect on the paths influenced by your loss—what strengths did you gain? What values were highlighted? Now, look forward. Envision yourself walking a new path, carrying forward the wisdom and love from your past experiences. What does this path look like? How does it feel to acknowledge your past but also to embrace the potential of your future? This visualization can help reinforce the Stoic practice of using loss as a stepping stone for growth and renewal.

By integrating these Stoic principles into our lives, we equip ourselves not only to survive the crises of loss but to emerge from them with greater resilience and clarity. Through the practice of Stoic reflection, the acceptance of life's impermanence, and courageously facing our grief, we find the strength to continue our journey with renewed purpose and wisdom. As we move forward, let us carry with us the lessons of Stoicism—not as mere spectators of our fate but as active participants in shaping a life of virtue and meaning, even in the wake of loss.

STOIC STRATEGIES FOR COPING WITH UNEXPECTED CHANGE

Change is as much a part of life's fabric as the seasons that cycle from spring to winter. Stoic philosophy, with its deep roots in understanding and adapting to the impermanence of life, teaches us to view change not as an anomaly but as an inherent aspect of the human experience. This perspective is crucial because it helps prepare us for the inevitable shifts we will encounter, from negligible alterations in our daily routines to significant transformations in our personal and professional lives. By framing change as a natural and expected element of living, Stoicism arms us with the mental and emotional skills needed to face new circumstances with a composed and measured response rather than resistance or fear.

Developing cognitive flexibility is essential in adapting to change effectively. This trait, which involves the ability to adjust one's thinking and behavior in response to new information or environments, is highly valued in Stoic practice. It allows us to remain open and adaptable in the face of life's constant changes. Cognitive flexibility can be cultivated through various strategies that challenge our existing beliefs and open us up to new perspectives and experiences. For instance, engaging with diverse viewpoints, whether through reading, conversation, or travel, can broaden our understanding and reduce the rigidity of our preconceptions. Another effective method is to practice scenario planning, where you envision different outcomes and strategize various responses. This not only prepares you for potential changes but also reduces anxiety about the unknown, as you've mentally equipped yourself to handle multiple possibilities.

Stoicism isn't just about personal resilience; it's deeply woven with virtues that guide our responses to every aspect of life, including change. The Stoic virtues of courage and wisdom are particularly pertinent when navigating through new phases. Courage in Stoicism involves more than bravery in the face of danger; it's about the moral courage to embrace change and the uncertainty it brings. It's about seeing the growth potential in new challenges and stepping forward with confidence, even when the path isn't obvious. Wisdom, on the other hand, helps us make decisions that are not based on fleeting emotions or superficial judgments but are rooted in a deep understanding of our values and the broader context of our lives. It enables us to discern which changes are beneficial and align with our long-term goals and which are distractions that lead us astray.

Practical steps are necessary for adapting to new circumstances effectively. Setting small, manageable goals is a powerful strategy during times of change. These goals can act as stepping stones that guide your path through unfamiliar territory, providing a sense of direction and accomplishment that bolsters your confidence and motivation. For example, if you're transitioning to a new career field, your initial goals might include networking with professionals in the industry or completing specific skill-building courses. Additionally, seeking support from Stoic communities or like-minded individuals can provide both practical advice and emotional encouragement. These communities, whether found in local meetups or online forums, offer a wealth of collective wisdom and experience that can be invaluable in navigating change. They remind us that we are not alone in our struggles and that shared human understanding is a reservoir from which we can all draw strength and insight.

By integrating these strategies into our lives, we not only equip ourselves to manage the inevitable changes that come our way but also transform our experience of these changes from something we have to endure into opportunities for personal growth and renewal. Through the mindful application of Stoic teachings—embracing change as a natural part of life, cultivating cognitive flexibility, leaning on core Stoic virtues, and taking practical steps for adaptation—we can navigate life's uncertainties not just with resilience but with a proactive enthusiasm that turns every change into a stepping stone towards a richer, more fulfilling life.

MAINTAINING A STOIC MINDSET DURING GLOBAL UNCERTAINTY

In a world where headlines often herald crises—from financial downturns to environmental disasters—the need to maintain a stoic mindset becomes not just helpful but essential. Stoicism teaches the art of living in the present moment, a skill that becomes particularly valuable during times of global uncertainty. By focusing our mental energy on the present, we shield ourselves from the paralyzing effects of worry about future events that are beyond our control. This practice is rooted in the understanding that anxiety often stems from hypothetical scenarios that may never materialize. Instead, Stoicism encourages us to engage directly with the here and now—where we can make actual, not imagined, differences.

Living in the present moment involves a conscious awareness of our current experiences and actions. It means acknowledging our feelings about global events but choosing not to be overwhelmed by uncertain future implications. For instance, consider the approach of a Stoic during an economic recession. Instead of being consumed by worry about potential job loss, the Stoic would focus on enhancing their current job performance and perhaps even taking steps to improve their skills, making themselves more valuable in the workplace. This focus on present actions allows for a sense of control and effectiveness that future-oriented worry never could.

Engagement in proactive behaviors is another fundamental aspect of maintaining a Stoic mindset in times of global uncertainty. Stoics are not passive observers of life; they are active participants who manage their actions within their sphere of influence. Staying informed about international events, preparing for reasonable outcomes, and contributing positively to one's community are all proactive behaviors endorsed by Stoicism. For example, in the face of an impending natural disaster, a Stoic would focus on preparing their home and helping neighbors secure their properties. By concentrating on these actionable steps, they maintain a sense of personal agency and community responsibility, which are crucial to Stoic ethics.

The concept of Stoic acceptance plays a pivotal role in how we respond to global uncertainties. This acceptance is not about resignation or passivity; instead, it's about acknowledging the reality of a situation without letting it dictate our inner state. Acceptance allows us to see the world as it is, not as we wish it to be, and this clarity of vision enables us to act more effectively. When we accept that certain aspects of global events are beyond our control, we can direct our energies towards more fruitful endeavors—those within our power to change. This Stoic acceptance can be particularly empowering in environmental activism, where the scale of global challenges can seem daunting. Activists who embrace Stoic principles focus their efforts on achievable projects and community education, thus making tangible impacts without becoming overwhelmed by the broader issues beyond their control.

Historical examples abound of Stoics who maintained their composure and integrity in the face of significant societal challenges. One poignant instance is Cato the Younger, a Roman statesman who often found himself at odds with Julius Caesar. Despite the upheaval and the personal risk of opposing Caesar, Cato remained steadfastly committed to his principles, embodying Stoic virtues such as courage and justice. His life, particularly his refusal to compromise his ethical standards despite extreme pressure, offers a powerful lesson in maintaining moral integrity during times of political turmoil. In a more contemporary context, consider the calm persistence of individuals who continued to advocate for social justice and human rights even when faced with social backlash or indifference. Their resilience in the face of adversity is a modern reflection of Stoic endurance and commitment to virtue.

These narratives not only inspire but also guide us in applying Stoic principles to our own lives, especially in times of global uncertainty. By focusing on the present, engaging in proactive behaviors, practicing acceptance, and drawing inspiration from those who have navigated crises with Stoic grace, we, too, can cultivate a mindset that turns challenges into opportunities for growth and affirmation of our deepest values. In doing so, we uphold the Stoic ideal of living a life of purpose and resilience, regardless of the external circumstances we face.

THE STOIC'S PATH TO RECOVERY AND REBUILDING AFTER SETBACKS

In the Stoic view, setbacks are not mere obstacles or defeats; they are catalysts for growth and self-discovery. This perspective is fundamental to understanding how Stoicism transforms our approach to life's inevitable downturns. Unlike the common perception that setbacks are purely negative, Stoicism invites us to see them as valuable opportunities to practice virtues such as resilience, moderation, and wisdom. These moments challenge us not only to endure but to expand our capacities and fortify our character.

The initial phase of dealing with any setback involves a constructive response. Rather than succumbing to frustration or despair, Stoicism teaches us to engage with these challenges actively and thoughtfully. This engagement is not about quick fixes but about a deep, sustained commitment to learning from every experience. For instance, if a project at work fails to yield the expected results, instead of viewing this as a failure, a Stoic approach would be to analyze the process critically—what were the strengths, and what could be improved? This mindset shifts the focus from what went wrong to what we can learn, setting the stage for more effective future endeavors.

Rebuilding one's life or work after a setback is significantly enriched by the application of Stoic principles. Resilience, a critical Stoic virtue, involves more than mere endurance; it encompasses the ability to recover gracefully and emerge stronger. This resilience can be cultivated through regular reflection on personal experiences, assessing not just outcomes but the thought processes and decisions that led to those outcomes. Moderation plays a crucial role as well, helping to maintain balance amid the highs and lows of recovery. It guards against extremes of overconfidence or despair, promoting a steady and sustainable path forward. Wisdom, the third pillar, guides the decision-making process, ensuring that each step taken is aligned with one's deeper values and long-term objectives.

A practical approach to rebuilding after setbacks involves a structured, step-by-step roadmap that emphasizes long-term growth and continuous adaptation of Stoic principles. This roadmap might start with setting clear, achievable goals that build on the lessons learned from the setback. Each goal should be specific and have a time limit, providing a clear path for progress and reassessment. Regular reflection is crucial—this could be a weekly review of what was accomplished, what challenges were encountered, and how they were addressed. This practice not only ensures adherence to Stoic principles but also fosters a habit of mindful engagement with one's progress and setbacks.

Adaptation is another critical component of this roadmap. The Stoic practice of remaining open to new information and experiences allows for the flexibility needed to adjust plans as circumstances evolve. This dynamic approach ensures that strategies remain relevant and responsive to real-world conditions, enhancing the effectiveness of the recovery process. Additionally, the pursuit of virtue, which is central to Stoic philosophy, should permeate every stage of this roadmap. Whether in setting goals, reflecting on progress, or adapting strategies, the commitment to practicing virtues such as honesty, courage, and humility should guide all actions and decisions.

This structured yet flexible approach not only aids in recovery but also transforms the experience of dealing with setbacks. It shifts the narrative from one of recovery to one of opportunity—where each setback becomes a chance to refine strategies, strengthen virtues, and deepen understanding. This transformation is not about returning to a previous state but about reaching new heights of personal and professional development.

In essence, the Stoic's path to recovery and rebuilding is a journey marked by continuous learning, ethical growth, and strategic adaptation. It is a process that not only restores but enhances, guided by a philosophy that sees every challenge as a doorway to greater wisdom and strength. As we wrap up this exploration of Stoicism in times of crisis, let us carry forward the lessons learned here—not only to navigate setbacks when they arise but to transform them into profound opportunities for growth and renewal. These strategies, rooted in ancient wisdom, provide us with the tools not just to survive but to thrive, crafting lives of resilience, purpose, and deep fulfillment.

As we conclude this chapter, we reflect on the transformative power of Stoic philosophy in times of crisis. From finding strength in loss to navigating unexpected changes, from maintaining composure in global uncertainty to recovering from setbacks, Stoicism offers a comprehensive framework for facing life's challenges with grace and wisdom. Let us move forward, equipped with these timeless strategies, ready to turn every obstacle into an opportunity for growth. As we transition into the next chapter, we will delve deeper into the practical applications of Stoicism in everyday life, exploring how these ancient principles can be seamlessly integrated into modern living to enhance our resilience, happiness, and overall well-being.

THE INTERSECTION OF STOICISM
AND MODERN PSYCHOLOGY

A s you navigate through the ebb and flow of everyday life, have you ever wondered how ancient philosophical insights could effectively intersect with modern psychological practices to enhance your mental wellness? This curiosity unveils a profound connection between Stoicism, a philosophy rooted in logic and personal ethics, and Cognitive Behavioral Therapy (CBT), a modern psychological approach that emphasizes the importance of thought patterns in influencing behavior and emotional health. This chapter explores the symphony between these two disciplines, revealing how they collectively offer a robust framework for managing thoughts, emotions, and behaviors in a way that promotes a healthier, more resilient mental state.

COGNITIVE BEHAVIORAL THERAPY AND STOICISM: A COMPARISON

Outline Similarities in Principles

Both Stoicism and Cognitive Behavioral Therapy (CBT) pivot on a central insight: our feelings and behaviors are significantly shaped by our thoughts. Stoicism, established in the bustling marketplaces of ancient Greece, teaches that it is not events themselves that disturb people but the views they take of them. Similarly, CBT, developed in the mid-20th century, operates on the understanding that changing dysfunctional thinking patterns can alter emotions and behaviors, leading to improved mental health and greater life satisfaction.

The commonalities between these two approaches are striking. Stoicism encourages individuals to discern between what is within their control—mainly their thoughts, motives, and actions—and what is not, which includes the actions and opinions of others and external events. CBT also empowers individuals to identify and modify distorted thinking, focusing on managing worry and anxiety by addressing how thoughts influence emotions and behaviors. Both philosophies believe in a proactive rather than reactive approach to mental challenges, emphasizing personal responsibility and the power of self-reflection.

Discuss the Concept of Cognitive Distortion

Cognitive distortions are irrational thought patterns that often lead to negative emotions and behaviors. These are central to CBT's diagnostic approach, where therapists help clients identify and challenge distorted thoughts. Stoicism, with its focus on perceptions, closely aligns with this concept. Stoics teach that by changing our perceptions, we can maintain serenity despite external circumstances. For instance, Epictetus famously said, "Men are disturbed not by things, but by the view which they take of them."

In practice, both Stoicism and CBT encourage individuals to engage in cognitive restructuring—a process of identifying and disputing irrational or dysfunctional thoughts. Stoicism uses techniques like the premeditation of evils, which involves contemplating potential adverse outcomes to diminish the distress they cause. At the same time, CBT employs similar strategies, such as worst-case scenario planning, helping individuals to assess and prepare realistically for potential challenges.

Provide Comparative Techniques

To illustrate the synergy between Stoicism and CBT, consider the technique of negative visualization, a Stoic exercise that involves contemplating the loss of things valued to reduce distress when such losses occur. Similarly, CBT's worst-case scenario technique encourages individuals to face their fears by visualizing the worst possible outcome and rationally planning responses, thereby reducing anxiety and increasing preparedness.

Both approaches also emphasize the importance of daily practice in developing mental resilience. For instance, Marcus Aurelius, a Stoic philosopher, kept a personal journal to reflect on and challenge his thoughts, a method akin to CBT's use of thought records where clients track dysfunctional thoughts and their emotional consequences to identify patterns and triggers.

Evaluate Effectiveness in Therapy

The integration of Stoic principles into CBT has been evidenced to enhance therapeutic outcomes, particularly in treating anxiety and depression. Studies indicate that individuals who employ Stoic practices such as focusing on the controllable, accepting the inevitable, and practicing mindfulness report lower levels of stress and higher life satisfaction. Clinical observations also suggest that incorporating Stoic exercises into CBT sessions helps clients manage emotional disturbances better, fostering a more balanced and proactive approach to mental health challenges.

The convergence of Stoicism and Cognitive Behavioral Therapy offers a compelling toolkit for anyone seeking to understand and improve their mental health. By grounding modern psychological practices in Stoic wisdom, individuals are equipped with a time-tested yet scientifically supported framework for navigating the complexities of the mind, ensuring a journey toward greater emotional resilience and psychological well-being. As we delve deeper into the practical applications of this synergy, you may discover not only the science of mental health but also the art of living well.

STOICISM AND MINDFULNESS: TECHNIQUES FOR THE PRESENT MOMENT

Mindfulness, in both psychological and Stoic contexts, revolves around the cultivation of a heightened state of awareness and presence in the current moment. Psychologically, mindfulness is viewed as the practice of being attentively present and consciously aware of our thoughts, emotions, and environment without judgment or distraction. In Stoicism, mindfulness aligns closely with the concept of Prosoche, which is the practice of attentive and vigilant self-awareness of one's thoughts and actions in accordance with reason. Both disciplines hold that mindfulness is not merely a passive state but an active pursuit of clarity aimed at enhancing rational thinking and emotional equanimity.

The practice of mindfulness in modern psychology often involves meditation techniques that encourage individuals to observe their thoughts and feelings without attachment, thereby gaining greater control over their responses. Stoicism offers a parallel through exercises like the 'view from above,' where one visualizes one's life from a broader perspective, fostering a sense of the temporal and spatial smallness of one's concerns. This Stoic practice not only encourages a wider perspective but also diminishes the emotional impact of present worries, aligning closely with the psychological practice of mindfulness in reducing stress and anxiety.

Another Stoic practice, voluntary discomfort, involves intentionally placing oneself in uncomfortable situations to build resilience and reduce the fear of adversity. This could include fasting or taking cold showers. Similarly, in modern psychological practices, mindfulness might be cultivated through exposure to less comfortable situations to decrease sensitivity to stressors and increase the ability to manage them effectively. Both practices teach that discomfort can be a path to growth, reinforcing the idea that challenges should not be feared but used as opportunities for strengthening character and competence.

The benefits of mindfulness from a Stoic perspective converge on the concept of apatheia, or freedom from distress. By practicing mindfulness, you train yourself to detach from misleading perceptions and irrational impulses that can lead to distress. This Stoic goal is achieved by maintaining a focus on rational judgment and internal tranquility, irrespective of external circumstances. Modern psychological approaches echo this benefit, as mindfulness has been shown to significantly decrease symptoms in conditions such as depression, anxiety, and PTSD by helping individuals reframe their thoughts and reduce overwhelming emotional reactions.

For practical daily integration, consider starting with a simple mindfulness routine each morning. Spend a few minutes in quiet reflection, perhaps following the Stoic meditation on the dichotomy of control, focusing on distinguishing between what you can change and what you cannot. Throughout the day, take brief "mindfulness breaks" to assess your current state of mind. Ask yourself questions like, "Are my responses aligned with my values? Am I focusing on the present or worrying about the past or future?" These check-ins can help recenter your thoughts and ensure you are living true to Stoic principles and psychological best practices for mental well-being.

Incorporating these mindfulness techniques into your routine not only enhances your ability to live in the present but also fortifies your resilience against the stresses of daily life. Whether you are facing a challenging situation at work or navigating complex personal relationships, mindfulness offers a toolset that empowers you to manage your thoughts and emotions with clarity and purpose. By fostering a habit of mindful living, guided by both Stoic wisdom and psychological practices, you cultivate a life characterized by increased rationality, emotional stability, and overall serenity.

THE PSYCHOLOGICAL BENEFITS OF STOIC ACCEPTANCE

Acceptance, a concept both respected and vital within the realms of psychology and Stoic philosophy, serves as a cornerstone in managing psychological distress. In the psychological context, acceptance is often associated with therapies like Acceptance and Commitment Therapy (ACT), which emphasizes accepting whatever is out of personal control while committing to actions that enrich life. In Stoicism, acceptance is deeply ingrained in the philosophy's teachings, focusing on acknowledging the limits of our power over external events and only internalizing what we can influence—our perceptions, actions, and will.

Both Stoicism and ACT advocate for a form of acceptance that is active rather than passive. It's not about resigning oneself to fate but rather about recognizing the futility in resisting the unchangeable, thus channeling one's energy more productively. This form of acceptance is not about giving up but is an empowering state of acknowledging reality as it is, which paradoxically enables more significant change in one's life. Stoic acceptance, for instance, teaches that we should not be upset by the events themselves but rather by our opinions about them. This is echoed in ACT, which suggests that suffering comes less from the experience itself and more from our entangled reactions to the experience.

Embracing Stoic acceptance can lead to decreased emotional responsiveness. For example, consider someone dealing with chronic pain. A Stoic approach would be to urge this individual not to focus on the unfairness of the pain or the limitations it imposes but instead on their ability to respond to the pain with dignity and courage. This shift in focus from the uncontrollable (the existence of pain) to the controllable (the response to pain) can lead to significant decreases in emotional disturbances like anger and depression, thereby fostering superior emotional equilibrium.

Moreover, Stoic acceptance enhances resilience by cultivating an attitude of equanimity towards life's ups and downs. It teaches that while we cannot control external events, we can control our perceptions and reactions, which in turn shape our reality. This view is crucial during significant life transitions, such as during the loss of a loved one. In such times, Stoic acceptance helps individuals navigate their grief by allowing them to experience their emotions without being overwhelmed by them. It encourages the bereaved to appreciate the time they had with the person and to accept the loss as part of the natural course of life, thus supporting a healthier grieving process.

One effective exercise to cultivate Stoic acceptance involves the practice of imagining life without a loved, cherished possession or even personal ability. This visualization not only prepares one for potential losses but also enhances appreciation for the present, fostering a mindset that is more resistant to disturbances when changes occur. This method, known as negative visualization, is not about pessimism; instead, it's about tempering the soul to face any of life's realities without despair.

Another strategy involves systematic exposure to personal fears or discomforts. For instance, if one fears public speaking, the Stoic practice would involve gradually exposing oneself to speaking in front of others, starting with small, supportive groups and slowly increasing the audience size. This practice not only reduces the fear over time but also empowers the individual, reinforcing their capacity to handle previously daunting situations.

In these ways, Stoic acceptance serves as a powerful tool in the psychological toolkit, offering strategies that lead to a life characterized not by avoidance of hardship but by graceful acceptance and proactive engagement with the world. Through these practices, you learn to hold a calm center, even as the storms of life rage around you, ensuring that when changes come, you are not uprooted.

RESILIENCE TRAINING: PSYCHOLOGICAL INSIGHTS FROM STOIC EXERCISES

Resilience, a term frequently spotlighted in both psychological circles and Stoic discussions, encapsulates more than just the ability to recover from setbacks; it involves a profound capacity to adapt and thrive regardless of difficulties. From a psychological perspective, resilience is often defined as the ability to bounce back from adversity, maintaining functional psychological and physical baseline levels. Stoicism, however, enriches this understanding by emphasizing not only the capacity to endure but also the ability to preserve virtue and steadfastness under pressure. This nuanced view suggests that resilience is not merely about returning to a former state but evolving through challenges in a way that aligns with one's ethical values.

Often, Stoic practices that foster resilience involve exercises that push the individual beyond their comfort zone, thus fortifying their mental and emotional defenses. One such practice is voluntary hardship, which includes intentionally engaging in challenging activities like fasting, sleeping on the floor, or avoiding comforts like air conditioning. These practices are not masochistic but are designed to strengthen one's fortitude against future hardships, much like a muscle grows stronger through exertion. Another key Stoic exercise is reflective contemplation, where one reviews one's day to evaluate one's responses to various challenges. This practice cultivates a mindful awareness of one's reactions and promotes a habit of learning from every situation.

These Stoic exercises share a striking resemblance with modern psychological resilience training programs. Such programs often incorporate elements such as exposure to controlled stressors, which help individuals develop coping strategies and reduce sensitivity to anxiety triggers. Similarly, reflective processing—akin to

Stoic contemplation—urges individuals to learn from past experiences, thereby enhancing their ability to handle future stresses more effectively.

Various studies and observations support the effectiveness of integrating Stoic practices into resilience training. For instance, research within military training environments, where resilience is critical, has shown that soldiers exposed to pre-deployment training that includes Stoic principles, such as controlling focus under pressure and maintaining mental clarity in chaos, perform better in high-stress situations. Similarly, high-stress occupations such as emergency services have benefited from resilience training that incorporates Stoic exercises, helping professionals maintain calm and effective responses in crises.

In sports psychology, the incorporation of Stoic practices, like focusing only on controllable aspects of the game, has been linked to improved performance and mental endurance among athletes. These individuals learn to maintain focus during competitions, manage anxiety, and maintain a performance-enhancing mindset despite the high-pressure environment. This Stoic approach helps athletes not only during the event but in their overall mental preparedness and recovery from setbacks, whether they are injuries or losses.

Incorporating these Stoic resilience-building practices into your daily life can simply start, for instance, by choosing to practice voluntary hardship—skipping a meal or turning off your electronic devices for several hours one day a week. Reflect on this experience at the end of the day, noting any feelings of discomfort and your reactions to them. Over time, these small exercises can significantly enhance your resilience, preparing you for more significant life challenges and enabling a more stoic response to adversity.

By integrating Stoic exercises into modern resilience training, you tap into a wellspring of historical wisdom that complements contemporary psychological practices. This synergy not only enriches our understanding of resilience but also broadens the tools available for developing this crucial trait. Through these practices, you are not just equipped to handle the inevitable difficulties of life but also emerge from them more assertive, virtuous, and steadfast.

In this exploration of resilience from both Stoic and psychological viewpoints, we've uncovered how ancient practices can bolster modern mental fitness. As we transition from understanding individual resilience to exploring community resilience in the next chapter, remember that the principles of Stoicism extend beyond personal development. They also offer a blueprint for building stronger, more supportive communities that can withstand and thrive through collective challenges.

STOICISM AND THE PURSUIT OF HAPPINESS

I n the midst of life's relentless pace, where the pursuit of 'happiness' often leads us down paths of fleeting pleasures and superficial achievements, how do we anchor our happiness in something more enduring and less vulnerable to life's inevitable fluctuations? Stoicism, a philosophical beacon from antiquity, offers a profound and lasting interpretation of happiness that challenges the conventional chase for ephemeral delights, guiding us instead towards a life of virtue and internal contentment.

DEFINING HAPPINESS IN STOIC TERMS

Happiness, or 'Eudaimonia' as we know it in Stoic philosophy, transcends the modern interpretation of fleeting emotional highs or the accumulation of material successes. Instead, it is conceived as the profound joy that arises from living a life aligned with virtue and rationality. This Stoic happiness is cultivated through deliberate ethical living and self-mastery, making it almost impervious to external circumstances and vicissitudes.

The distinction between Stoic happiness and hedonistic pleasure is pivotal. Hedonism, which advocates the pursuit of pleasure and the avoidance of pain, often results in happiness that relies upon external conditions—thus, it is inherently unstable and fleeting. Stoicism criticizes this dependence on external sources for happiness, proposing instead that true contentment comes from within, from living a life according to nature's rational order and one's rational nature.

A unique aspect of Stoic philosophy is the concept of 'preferred indifferents.' These are external things—such as wealth, health, and reputation—that, while not necessary for happiness, can be pursued and enjoyed if one acquires them in a manner that does not compromise one's virtue. The Stoics teach that while these 'indifferents' may facilitate a comfortable life, they should never be the source of our happiness, nor should their loss or absence be a source of great distress. This perspective inspires a balanced approach to life's external offerings, appreciating and utilizing them without becoming overly attached or dependent.

The lives of notable Stoics such as Seneca and Epictetus exemplify this approach to happiness. Seneca, a wealthy man by any standard, used his resources to foster his philosophical pursuits yet remained detached from the wealth itself, often writing about the virtues of simplicity and the dangers of affluence. Epictetus, born into slavery, found his freedom not through external emancipation —which he eventually did receive—but through his determined focus on internal growth and understanding. Both figures demonstrated that Stoic happiness is achieved not through the possession of material goods or favorable circumstances but through the cultivation of virtue, wisdom, and inner resilience.

Visual Element: Stoic Tree of Virtue and Happiness

The Stoic Tree of Virtue and Happiness (Infographic)

- Roots: Core Stoic Virtues (Wisdom, Courage, Justice, Temperance)
- Trunk: Stoic Practices (Reflection, Discipline, Mindfulness)
- Branches: Preferred Indifferents (Wealth, Health, Success)
- Leaves: Eudaimonia (Joy and Contentment derived from Virtuous Living)

This visual metaphor illustrates how the robust 'roots' of Stoic virtues support the enduring 'trunk' of daily Stoic practices, which in turn bear the 'leaves' of true happiness, irrespective of the 'branches' of external circumstances that may sway in the winds of fortune.

Through Stoicism, we reexamine our understanding of happiness, prompting a shift from seeking external validation or fleeting pleasures to fostering an inner citadel of virtue and wisdom. As we align our lives with these Stoic principles, we discover that true happiness is not something that is chased and caught; it is cultivated and lived, a byproduct of a life well-lived in accordance with reason and virtue. This Stoic happiness, deeply rooted and nourished by ethical living, offers not only personal peace but also enriches the world around us, making it a profound goal worthy of pursuit.

DAILY STOIC PRACTICES TO ENHANCE LIFE SATISFACTION

In the pursuit of a life marked not just by success but by deep fulfillment and calm, Stoicism offers not just a philosophy but a daily practice. Integrating Stoic exercises into your daily routine isn't just about adhering to an ancient philosophy—it's about creating a life that's more reflective, responsive, and rich in contentment. For those looking to infuse their day-to-day lives with the wisdom of Stoicism, several practices can be seamlessly incorporated into even the busiest schedules.

Morning meditations on gratitude are a cornerstone of daily Stoic practice. This exercise involves taking a few quiet moments each morning to reflect on what you are thankful for. It could range from appreciating the simple comfort of a home to acknowledging a loved one's support or even valuing the challenges that provide opportunities for growth. This practice sets an attitude of positivity and appreciation for the day ahead, anchoring you in a mindset that values what you have rather than what you lack. The Stoic emphasis on gratitude is profound because it shifts focus from external desires to internal wealth, fostering a sense of abundance that is not contingent on material possessions or status.

Evening reviews of actions are equally crucial. This practice involves taking time at the end of the day to reflect on your actions and decisions. Did they align with your Stoic values? How did you respond to stress or an unexpected challenge? Did you act out of impulse or from a place of reasoned decision-making? This introspection not only aids in personal growth by highlighting areas of improvement but also reinforces your commitment to living stoically. Over time, this routine nurtures a reflective mind that naturally leans towards making more considered and honorable choices.

Mindfulness during routine tasks is another practical Stoic exercise. It involves being fully present and engaged in the current activity without judgment or distraction. Whether you're washing dishes, driving, or typing an email, mindfulness turns these ordinary tasks into moments of meditation and presence. This practice deepens your connection to the present moment—a key Stoic aim —helping you cultivate a life where peace isn't something you seek from external sources but instead is something you generate from within.

Integrating Stoicism into Modern Life

Modern life, with its rapid pace and constant connectivity, can often feel at odds with the thoughtful, deliberate practice of Stoicism. However, there are numerous ways to weave Stoic exercises into the fabric of contemporary living. For instance, use your breaks at work to practice brief reflections or mindfulness exercises. Just a few minutes of focusing on your breath or contemplating a Stoic principle can reset your mind and reduce stress. Your commute can be transformed into an educational session by listening to audiobooks or podcasts on Stoicism, turning traffic jams into opportunities for learning and reflection.

Another tip is to set reminders on your phone or computer for Stoic reflections. These can be simple prompts, like "What are you grateful for?" or "What is within your control?" popping up throughout your day to realign your focus with Stoic ideals. This method ensures that Stoicism isn't just something you read about or think about in abstract terms—it becomes a lived experience integrated into the workings of daily life.

Success Stories

The transformative impact of these Stoic practices is not just theoretical. Many individuals have reported significant enhancements in their life satisfaction after integrating Stoicism into their daily routines. Take, for instance, a corporate lawyer who started practicing morning gratitude meditations. She reported a noticeable decrease in her usual stress levels and an increase in her overall job satisfaction. She attributed these changes to her newfound ability to appreciate her achievements and the positive aspects of her challenging job. Another example is a stay-at-home parent who found that practicing mindfulness during routine tasks helped manage the day-to-day stresses of parenting, making him more present and patient.

These testimonies underscore a crucial truth about Stoicism: it is profoundly practical. Its practices are designed not just for the quiet of meditation rooms or the isolation of retreats but for the rough and tumble of everyday life. They provide tools to transform not just how you think but how you live, bringing a depth of satisfaction that endures beyond changing circumstances and fleeting pleasures. As you continue to explore and integrate these practices into your daily life, you may find that Stoicism offers not just a philosophy or a set of practices but a roadmap to a highly fulfilling way of living.

BALANCING AMBITION AND CONTENTMENT: A STOIC PERSPECTIVE

Ambition and contentment might seem like opposing forces, yet Stoicism presents a unique framework where both can coexist harmoniously, enriching one's life rather than pulling it apart. The

Stoic approach to ambition does not dismiss it but instead refines its direction and purpose. It encourages the pursuit of excellence and meaningful goals, but crucially, these goals are to be pursued in alignment with virtuous living and ethical principles. This perspective ensures that ambition does not overrun ethical considerations or personal integrity, keeping us grounded in what truly enriches our lives.

In the realm of Stoicism, ambition is viewed as a positive force when it drives us to improve ourselves and contribute to the world in meaningful ways. However, this improvement and contribution must always adhere to Stoic virtues such as wisdom, justice, courage, and moderation. For instance, ambition that leads to cutthroat competition or unethical behaviors for personal gain is unambiguously against Stoic values. Instead, Stoics advocate for ambitions that elevate not only the individual but also those around them, fostering a collective well-being.

The balance between ambition and contentment is also maintained by embracing contentment with the present. While it's natural to strive for future goals, finding joy in the current moment and appreciating what we already have is equally important. This does not mean complacency or abandoning future aspirations but recognizing and valuing the richness of the present. Such contentment is cultivated through gratitude, mindfulness, and acceptance—practices that anchor us amidst the often tumultuous pursuit of our goals. By fostering contentment with the present, we protect ourselves from the disenchantment that can come if ambitions are delayed or derailed. It helps maintain an internal balance, ensuring that our well-being does not become dependent on external achievements.

Reflective goal-setting is a practical Stoic tool that bridges ambition with virtue. This involves setting goals that are not only ambitious but reflective of Stoic virtues, ensuring that our pursuits contribute positively to our character and overall happiness. When setting goals, ask yourself: Are these goals fostering my growth in virtue? Are they benefiting others as much as they benefit me? This reflective practice turns goal-setting into a disciplined exercise of self-awareness and ethical scrutiny, aligning our ambitions with our deepest values and ensuring that our pursuits are not just about reaching a destination but about enriching the journey there with integrity and purpose.

The lives of both historical and contemporary figures who have successfully balanced ambition with contentment offer inspiring illustrations of this Stoic ideal in action. Consider the story of Cato the Younger, a figure renowned in Stoic tradition for his unwavering integrity. Cato's political ambitions were driven by a deep commitment to the Roman Republic's ideals, advocating for justice and the rule of law despite the personal risks these stances entailed. His life demonstrates how ambition, when guided by staunch ethical principles, can pursue noble ends, even in the face of personal loss or failure.

In contemporary times, we see similar embodiments of Stoic balance in individuals like Malala Yousafzai, whose ambition for educational equality deeply intertwines with her commitment to peace and justice. Despite immense challenges and threats, her goals remain steadfastly aligned with her virtues, inspiring millions worldwide. Her journey underscores the fact that true ambition, informed by Stoic principles, looks beyond personal achievement to the broader impact of one's actions on the community and the world.

This Stoic approach to balancing ambition with contentment invites us to rethink our pursuits and the values that underpin them. It inspires us to aim high but with a foundation firmly rooted in virtue and ethical living. As you reflect on your ambitions and the contentment you derive from your present, consider how you can weave them together through Stoic wisdom, not only to achieve external success but to cultivate a life of profound internal richness and peace.

THE ROLE OF COMMUNITY AND RELATIONSHIPS IN STOIC HAPPINESS

In the tapestry of Stoic philosophy, the threads of community and relationships are not merely decorative but structurally vital. Stoicism, often misconstrued as a doctrine of personal endurance and detached rationality, places profound importance on the fabric of community and the quality of our relationships. This emphasis is rooted in the belief that virtues like justice and charity are not practiced in isolation but portray our interactions with others. The Stoic concept of internationalism extends this idea on a global scale, advocating for a worldview where every human interaction is an opportunity to practice these virtues, treating all individuals with fairness and kindness regardless of their cultural or geographical distinctions.

This Stoic principle of internationalism is not just an ideal but a practical approach to living. It encourages viewing oneself as a citizen of the world, which fosters a sense of responsibility towards fellow humans regardless of one's immediate social or cultural circles. This broadened perspective helps to cultivate a sense of connectedness and empathy, reducing prejudices and promoting a more inclusive approach to social interactions. By embracing this global citizenship, you not only expand your own social and emotional horizons but also contribute to a more harmonious and understanding world.

Engaging in healthy relationships and community activities offers fertile ground for practicing Stoic virtues. Each interaction, whether it's volunteering at a local shelter, participating in a community clean-up, or simply lending an empathetic ear to a friend, serves as a practical application of Stoic teachings. These activities provide real-life scenarios where you can cultivate virtues like charity, justice, and temperance. For instance, volunteering allows for the practice of charity and empathy, pushing you to consider the well-being of others and offering your skills and time for their benefit. Similarly, resolving conflicts within your community or family with fairness and patience allows you to practice justice and temperance, balancing your own emotions and judgments with the needs and views of others.

Stoicism teaches that you will not achieve true happiness —Eudaimonia—through solitary pursuit but through contributions to the welfare of others, which in turn enriches our own lives. This reciprocal enhancement of contentment is evident in relationships that rely on principles of mutual respect, understanding, and support. Healthy relationships foster a supportive environment where individuals feel valued and connected, which significantly contributes to overall life satisfaction and resilience. These relationships become the channels through which Stoic virtues are not only practiced but also received, creating a cycle of positive interactions and personal growth.

Guidelines for Fostering Community Connections

Building and maintaining relationships that reflect Stoic principles is both a rewarding and challenging endeavor. Here are some practical guidelines to foster such connections:

- Volunteer Regularly: Engage in community service or volunteer work that aligns with your values. This not only benefits others but also enriches your own life, providing perspective and deepening your sense of gratitude and purpose.
- Participate in Discussion Groups: Whether it's a book club, a philosophy discussion group, or a community meeting, participation in these groups offers opportunities to exchange ideas, challenge your perceptions, and gain insights from diverse perspectives.
- Cultivate Open and Honest Communication: In your relationships, strive for transparency and honesty. This fosters trust and understanding, which are the essential components of any strong relationship.
- Practice Active Listening: Show genuine interest in others' thoughts and feelings. Active listening involves more than just hearing the words; it's about understanding the underlying emotions and intentions, which can significantly deepen interpersonal bonds.

By integrating these practices into your daily life, you actively contribute to a community where Stoic virtues are not just idealized but lived. Each act of kindness, each moment of honest interaction, and each decision made with fairness and consideration reverberates, influencing not only your happiness but also the well-being of the community at large.

As this chapter on the role of community and relationships in Stoic happiness concludes, we see how deeply interwoven our individual well-being is with the health of our relationships and communities. Stoicism, far from promoting solitary introspection, inspires active participation in the world—engaging with, learning from, and contributing to the community around us. This is not a divergence from the pursuit of personal happiness but a vital part of it, enriching our lives with depth, purpose, and joy.

In the next chapter, we will explore how the principles of Stoicism can be applied to modern ethical dilemmas, providing a Stoic lens through which to view and address some of the most pressing issues facing our world today.

ADVANCED STOIC WISDOM

As you delve deeper into the rich tapestry of Stoicism, you encounter intriguing contradictions that challenge the surface-level understanding of this philosophical stronghold. Imagine standing at a crossroads where paths marked by seemingly opposing signs—'Freedom in Chains' and 'Wealth in Want'—intersect. Here lies the fascinating dominion of Stoic paradoxes, profound statements that at first glance appear contradictory yet reveal deeper truths upon closer examination. These paradoxes are not mere wordplay but are designed to provoke thought, challenge conventional wisdom, and deepen your understanding of Stoic philosophy.

NAVIGATING THE STOIC PARADOXES

Stoicism presents several paradoxes that may initially puzzle the uninitiated. Consider the statement, "the sage is free while in chains," or "true wealth consists in having few wants." To the modern mind, accustomed to equating freedom with physical liberty and wealth with material abundance, these assertions might seem contradictory, even irrational. However, these paradoxes serve a critical function in Stoic philosophy, pushing you to reconsider your assumptions about what it means to be free, wealthy, or happy.

The first paradox, "the sage is free while in chains," challenges the conventional notion of freedom. In Stoicism, true freedom is not about external circumstances but about one's internal state. A sage, or a wise person fully practicing Stoic principles, remains free even in physical bondage because their peace and happiness are not reliant on external conditions but are rooted in their virtuous character and rational mind. This idea encourages you to reflect on the nature of your own freedoms. Are they dependent on external validations and conditions, or are they grounded in something more profound and more enduring within you?

Similarly, the paradox "wealth consists in having few wants" turns the typical understanding of wealth on its head. Stoicism teaches that true wealth comes not from an abundance of possessions but from a paucity of desires. By limiting your desires to what is necessary and within your control, you achieve a kind of wealth that is impervious to external fluctuations. This paradox prompts you to evaluate your desires and consumption habits. Are they contributing to genuine happiness and fulfillment, or are they merely chaining you to endless cycles of wanting and acquiring?

Philosophical Interpretations

Various Stoic thinkers have offered insights into these paradoxes. Epictetus, for instance, emphasized the liberating power of self-control and rationality, suggesting that one can be 'free' in any circumstance if one maintains control over one's thoughts and desires. Seneca, on the other hand, broadly explored the concept of wealth, arguing that true riches entail wisdom, virtue, and peace of mind—qualities that are not diminished by external poverty.

These interpretations underline a common theme in Stoic thought: the redefinition of conventional values to align with virtue and rationality. By understanding these philosophical elucidations, you gain not only a more profound comprehension of Stoic paradoxes but also practical guidance on embodying Stoic principles in your daily life.

Encouraging Reflective Engagement

To engage more with these paradoxes, consider incorporating them into your reflective practices. Journaling, for example, can be an excellent way to explore these concepts. Dedicate a section of your journal to pondering these paradoxes. Write about times when you felt 'free' despite external constraints, or reflect on what 'wealth' truly means to you. How do these reflections change your perspective on freedom and wealth?

Additionally, joining or forming discussion groups can provide diverse perspectives on these paradoxes, enriching your understanding and application of Stoic principles. These conversations can challenge your viewpoints, deepen your insights, and help you see practical ways to integrate Stoic wisdom into your life.

Navigating the paradoxes of Stoicism not only enhances your understanding of this philosophical tradition but also enriches your personal and spiritual growth. By challenging orthodox definitions of freedom, wealth, and happiness, Stoicism invites you on a transformative path where wisdom and virtue illuminate the journey, offering a richer, deeper sense of fulfillment that transcends the superficial and fleeting pleasures of the material world.

ADVANCED TECHNIQUES IN STOIC MEDITATION AND REFLECTION

As you progress in your Stoic practice, you may find yourself seeking more advanced and nuanced ways to engage with this ancient philosophy. Progressive techniques in Stoic meditation and reflection offer profound avenues to enhance your sense of connectedness to the world and deepen your understanding of yourself. One such practice is the contemplation of the cosmos, a meditation that extends your perspective beyond the proximity of daily concerns and fosters a profound sense of humility and belonging to a larger order.

Contemplation of the cosmos involves visualizing the vastness of the universe and your tiny, albeit significant, place within it. This practice not only puts the scale of human affairs into perspective but also aligns with the Stoic principle that everything is interconnected. By recognizing your part in the grand tapestry of existence, you cultivate a sense of gratitude and responsibility towards it. Such meditations are not just exercises in humility; they are reminders of our duty to live virtuously, as our actions contribute to the harmony or discord of the universe. To practice this, you might begin by visualizing the Earth from space, seeing it as a single point of light among many, and gradually expanding your view to include the stars and galaxies. Try to reflect on the interconnectedness of all things and the small yet significant role you play in this vast cosmos.

Another advanced technique involves the use of visualization to solidify Stoic principles in your character. Imagining yourself as the ideal Stoic sage can be a powerful exercise in embodying the virtues you aspire to. Picture how a sage would handle the situations you face: their calmness, their rationality, their kindness. Then, visualize yourself acting in the same way. This practice not only provides a clear model to strive towards but also helps bridge the gap between theoretical understanding and practical application. Similarly, envisaging oneself facing and overcoming fears can reinforce courage and resilience. By mentally rehearsing your successful navigation of dreaded scenarios, you build confidence and psychologically prepare yourself to face the challenges ahead.

Deep reflection techniques also play a crucial role in advanced Stoic practice. Unlike daily reflections, which might focus on immediate reactions and events, deeper reflective practices involve a more thorough analysis of your progress in virtue. The philosophical diary is an essential tool in this regard. Instead of simple entries, this diary involves detailed examinations of your thoughts, actions, and their alignment with Stoic principles over more extended periods—weekly or monthly. This could include reflections on how well you maintained equanimity in stressful situations, how effectively you practiced justice in your interactions, or how you can better cultivate temperance in your desires and actions.

Connecting these practices to Stoic theories on psychology and ethics reveals their grounding in traditional thought while illustrating their evolution to address modern needs. Stoicism teaches that the development of virtue is the path to true happiness. Advanced meditation and reflection practices will deepen your engagement with these virtues and foster a transformation that is both profound and practical. By regularly engaging in these practices, you not only gain deeper insights into Stoic philosophy but also boost your ability to apply its teachings in everyday life, leading to a more thoughtful, balanced, and fulfilling existence.

THE STOIC RESPONSE TO MODERN ETHICAL DILEMMAS

In today's fast-evolving society, we grapple with ethical dilemmas that are complex and multifaceted, ranging from bioethical questions about genetic modifications to concerns about environmental sustainability and the moral intricacies of digital privacy. Stoicism, with its rich tradition of ethical reasoning, offers a robust framework for navigating these contemporary issues. By applying Stoic virtues—wisdom, justice, courage, and temperance —to modern dilemmas, you will find clarity and direction even in situations where the moral route seems obscured by competing interests and technological complexities.

Framing Bioethics Through Stoic Virtues

Consider the realm of bioethics, where advancements in genetic engineering and biotechnology present scenarios that our ancestors could scarcely have imagined. Stoicism teaches us to approach such challenges with wisdom and justice, balancing the potential benefits of scientific advancements with the ethical need to respect human dignity and the natural world. For instance, when considering the use of CRISPR technology for gene editing, Stoic wisdom could guide you in weighing the potential to eradicate hereditary diseases against the ethical implications of altering human genetics. The virtue of justice would demand an impartial consideration regarding who gets access to such technologies and the potential long-term impacts on society. In discussions or decision-making forums, advocating for policies that reflect not only scientific capabilities but also ethical responsibility embodies the Stoic commitment to virtue in the face of progress.

Environmental Ethics and Stoic Cosmopolitanism

Environmental concerns offer another area where Stoicism's principles are urgently needed. The Stoic view of cosmopolitanism —that all humans are citizens of the world—can be extended to include our stewardship of the planet. Applying Stoic justice involves advocating for actions that not only benefit individual communities but also contribute to global ecological balance. This could mean supporting sustainable practices that protect the environment and future generations, promoting a broader sense of responsibility and interconnectedness. Stoic courage comes into play when taking a stand against environmentally harmful practices, despite opposition from powerful interests or the apathy of convenience. Here, the Stoic is called to act with moral courage, championing the cause of environmental justice even when it is unpopular or economically challenging.

Navigating Digital Privacy with Stoic Principles

Digital privacy issues also call for a Stoic response. The rapid growth of digital technologies, while offering unprecedented connectivity and access to information, also raises significant concerns about privacy and the ethical use of data. Stoic wisdom guides you to discern the appropriate use of technology, balancing the benefits of digital innovation with the need to protect individual rights and freedoms. Temperance, or the virtue of moderation, plays a critical role in managing one's digital footprint, advocating for a balanced approach to technology that avoids the extremes of data exploitation or techno-phobia. By promoting policies and practices that safeguard personal information while supporting beneficial innovations, you embody Stoic virtues in addressing one of the most pressing moral dilemmas of our time.

Encouraging Active Ethical Practice

To actively engage with these dilemmas, Stoicism encourages not only reflection but also practical action. Consider implementing regular ethical audits in your professional and personal life, where you assess how well your actions align with your moral values. Such practices not only foster personal growth but also have a ripple effect, influencing others in your community and beyond. Engaging in community discussions or online forums about these issues can further your understanding and impact, allowing you to contribute Stoically to broader societal debates.

Stoicism, with its emphasis on virtue and rational discussion, provides a powerful lens through which to view and respond to modern ethical dilemmas. Whether navigating the complexities of bioethics, advocating for environmental justice, or managing digital privacy, the principles of Stoicism offer guidance that is both practical and profound, driving you to act not out of self-interest but in service of the greater good. By applying these timeless principles to contemporary issues, you continue the Stoic tradition of ethical engagement, promoting a more just, thoughtful, and virtuous society.

LONG-TERM STOICISM: SUSTAINING PRACTICE OVER A LIFETIME

Maintaining a Stoic practice throughout a lifetime presents its own unique set of challenges, which can vary significantly from one stage of life to another. One common issue you might encounter is a sense of doubt—doubt about the effectiveness of Stoicism in addressing new or evolving life circumstances or doubt stemming from the often foreseeable routine and complacency that can diminish the vibrancy of any long-practiced philosophy. Additionally, external pressures such as changes in personal relationships, career transitions, or significant global events can test the resilience of your Stoic practices. Furthermore, as you age and move through different phases of life, the significance and application of Stoic principles may seem to shift, requiring a flexible and adaptive approach to maintain their effectiveness.

To navigate these challenges and sustain your commitment to Stoicism, it is crucial to rejuvenate your practice regularly. One effective strategy is to delve back into the foundational texts of Stoicism. Re-reading the works of Marcus Aurelius, Seneca, and Epictetus can rekindle your enthusiasm and offer new insights that resonate with your current circumstances. Each reading at different stages of life can bring new meaning and perspective, deepening your understanding and appreciation of Stoic teachings.

Engaging with Stoic communities is another vital strategy. Whether it's participating in online forums, attending workshops, or joining local groups, connecting with others who are also walking the Stoic path can provide both inspiration and practical support. These communities offer a platform for sharing experiences and strategies, strengthening your practice through shared wisdom and encouragement. Additionally, assuming a teaching role within these communities can further solidify your understanding and commitment. Teaching others not only helps you clarify your own beliefs and practices but also provides a sense of purpose and fulfillment that comes from contributing to others' growth.

The practice of Stoicism is not static; it evolves as you grow and as your life circumstances change. What was impactful in your youth may take on a different significance in later years. Recognizing and embracing this dynamic nature of Stoic practice is the key to maintaining its importance and usefulness. For instance, while the focus in earlier years might be on harnessing ambition and managing external challenges, later years might shift towards reflecting on one's legacy and cultivating tranquility. Adapting your practice to these changing priorities and circumstances ensures that Stoicism continues to provide guidance and comfort throughout your life.

The lifelong benefits of sustained Stoic practice are profound. Stories from long-term practitioners often highlight a deep-seated sense of peace, resilience, and fulfillment that pervades their lives. They speak of a robust composure that buffers them against the vagaries of life and a clarity of purpose that guides their choices and interactions. These stories not only serve as a testament to the enduring power of Stoicism but also as a beacon to newer practitioners, illustrating the profound impact that Stoicism can have when integrated into one's life over the long term.

In this chapter, we have explored the challenges of maintaining a Stoic practice throughout life and discussed strategies to rejuvenate and adapt this practice to ensure its ongoing effectiveness and relevance. We've also considered how the evolving nature of Stoic practice reflects the changing stages and circumstances of life, providing a flexible framework that supports a lifetime of growth and fulfillment. As we transition to the next chapter, we will delve deeper into specific Stoic practices that can help you navigate the complexities of modern life, offering tools and strategies that are both practical and transformative. This exploration will not only supplement your understanding of Stoic philosophy but also improve your ability to apply its principles in a way that enriches your everyday life.

CREATING A STOIC MINDSET

In the tapestry of life, each thread—every decision, action, and thought—intertwines to form the intricate pattern of our existence. But how often do we pause to consider the quality of these threads or the mindfulness with which we weave them? Stoicism, a philosophy designed for living well, provides the basis upon which we can create a life of purpose, resilience, and tranquility. This chapter invites you to integrate Stoic mindfulness into your daily routine, transforming ordinary moments into opportunities for growth and reflection.

CULTIVATING STOIC MINDFULNESS THROUGHOUT THE DAY

Mindfulness, in the Stoic sense, is not merely an act of meditation but a continuous thread that runs through the fabric of our daily lives. It involves a conscious focus on the present moment, an acceptance of what it brings, and a commitment to embody Stoic virtues in every action. Integrating Stoic mindfulness into your daily activities begins with the easiest yet most profound technique: conscious breathing.

Consider this: each breath you take is a new beginning, a moment ripe with potential for clarity and calm. By focusing on your breath, you anchor yourself in the present, steering your mind away from the clutter of past regrets and future anxieties. This practice can be employed anytime, anywhere—from the quiet of your morning routine to the chaos of a busy workday. Picture yourself in a stressful meeting; as tensions rise, you turn your focus inward to your breath, each inhalation and exhalation a reminder of your ability to maintain serenity and think clearly, embodying the Stoic ideal of tranquility amidst turmoil.

Building on this foundation of conscious breathing, you can further enrich your Stoic practice by integrating focused attention into your everyday tasks. Whether you are typing an email, cooking a meal, or engaging in conversation, fully immerse yourself in the activity. This means observing each sensation and action with inquisitiveness and detachment, recognizing that these are tasks within your control, and your mindful engagement with them can transform mundane routines into acts of philosophical practice.

To maintain this mindful state throughout the day, consider setting up intermittent reminders for Stoic reflections. These can be simple alerts on your phone or sticky notes placed in your workspace, each prompting you to pause and reflect on a Stoic virtue or the dichotomy of control. For instance, a reminder might prompt you to reflect on the virtue of temperance before a lunch meeting, encouraging you to make choices that align with your values rather than impulses.

Encouraging the Practice of 'Stoic Pauses'

Another powerful technique to enhance your daily Stoicism is the practice of 'Stoic pauses.' These are deliberate, short breaks taken at regular intervals—perhaps hourly or between major tasks—during which you withdraw from outward activities to realign with your Stoic principles. During a Stoic pause, you might step away from your desk to reflect on the events of the past hour, assessing your responses and adjustments needed to align more closely with Stoic virtues. This practice is valuable in high-pressure environments where reactive decisions can lead to regrettable outcomes. By routinely readjusting your approach, you ensure that your actions continue to be thoughtful and consistent with Stoic wisdom.

The benefits of cultivating continuous Stoic mindfulness are manifold. Emotionally, it helps regulate your responses, reducing the intensity of adverse reactions to stress or provocation. Practically, it increases your resilience to daily stressors as you become better equipped to handle challenges with a calm and focused mind. In decision-making, mindfulness enhances your clarity, allowing you to make choices that are not only reactive to immediate circumstances but also reflective of long-term goals and values. Ultimately, the continuous practice of Stoic mindfulness enriches your life satisfaction, as it nurtures a deeper engagement with the present and a more harmonious alignment with your philosophical ideals.

Incorporating these Stoic practices into your daily life does not require monumental changes but relatively small, consistent adjustments to your focus and actions. As you weave mindfulness into the fabric of your daily activities, you transform ordinary moments into profound opportunities for growth, embodying the

Stoic ideals of wisdom, courage, justice, and temperance in all that you do.

THE IMPORTANCE OF ROUTINE AND DISCIPLINE IN STOICISM

In the realm of Stoicism, discipline is not merely a practice but the bedrock upon which the structure of a Stoic life is built. It is the discipline that enables the consistent application of Stoic principles, crafting a life marked by greater self-control, virtue, and, ultimately, peace. Stoicism teaches us that without discipline, our efforts to live a virtuous life are scattered and sporadic, susceptible to the caprices of circumstance and emotion. With discipline, however, we forge a steady path through life's ups and downs, our actions and thoughts deeply rooted in Stoic wisdom.

Imagine starting each day not as a series of random events but as a well-structured narrative, each chapter flowing seamlessly into the next, guided by the principles of wisdom, courage, justice, and temperance. This is the power of a Stoic routine. Such a routine might begin with the early morning hours dedicated to meditation, perhaps focusing on the day ahead and the virtues you wish to embody. This practice sets the tone for the day, grounding you in a state of mindfulness and purpose. Following meditation, a period of reflection on Stoic texts can provide philosophical guidance, connecting you with the timeless wisdom of Stoic sages like Marcus Aurelius or Seneca. These readings act not only as intellectual exercises but as spiritual sustenance, nourishing your inner life and preparing you for the day's challenges.

As the day unfolds, structured time for reflecting on your actions and their alignment with Stoic principles can help reinforce your commitment to living virtuously. This could be a midday review, a pause to assess the morning's events or an evening reflection, a quiet time to contemplate the day's successes and areas for improvement. Such practices ensure that your actions remain in harmony with your values, fostering a sense of integrity and consistency in your life. Additionally, scheduling regular periods to review and realign your actions with your goals and principles helps mitigate the impact of distractions and procrastination, common obstacles that can derail even the most dedicated practitioners.

ADDRESSING THE CHALLENGES OF MAINTAINING DISCIPLINE

Maintaining such a disciplined routine, however, is not without its challenges. The modern world, with its myriad distractions—from the incessant pings of smartphones to the constant demands of work and family life—can make sustained Stoic practice seem like a Herculean task. Procrastination, too, often creeps in, tempting us to defer our Stoic duties in favor of instantaneous pleasures or apparently urgent tasks. Yet, it is precisely in overcoming these challenges that the true value of Stoic discipline is revealed.

Stoic strategies to combat these distractions are both practical and philosophical. One effective method is the setting of distinct, manageable goals for each Stoic practice, whether it be meditation, reading, or reflection. By breaking down each practice into small, achievable steps, the overwhelming nature of sustaining discipline becomes more manageable, and the satisfaction of completing each step provides ongoing motivation. Furthermore, the Stoic practice of premeditatio malorum, or the premeditation of evils, can be adapted to anticipate potential distractions or reasons for procrastination. By foreseeing these challenges and planning your responses, you fortify your routine against the unforeseen, ensuring that your Stoic practices remain intact.

CASE STUDIES OF SUCCESSFUL STOIC ROUTINES

The effectiveness of these strategies is not merely theoretical but is evidenced by numerous individuals who have successfully integrated Stoic routines into their lives, reaping significant benefits. Consider the case of a high-level executive who, despite the hectic pace of corporate life, has maintained a morning routine of Stoic reflection and meditation for over a decade. This practice has not only enhanced his decision-making skills and resilience in the face of corporate challenges but has also improved his relationships with colleagues and family, imbuing his interactions with patience and understanding.

Another inspiring example is a teacher who incorporates Stoic principles into her daily interactions with students. By reflecting on Stoic virtues each morning and reviewing her day each evening, she has created a classroom environment that not only fosters academic excellence but also cultivates character and virtue among her students. Her disciplined adherence to Stoic practices has transformed her classroom into a space of growth and inquiry, benefiting both herself and her students.

These case studies highlight the transformative potential of a disciplined Stoic routine. By steadfastly applying Stoic principles through a structured daily schedule, individuals from all walks of life can achieve a more profound sense of fulfillment, resilience, and peace.

USING STOIC WISDOM TO SHAPE YOUR LIFE PHILOSOPHY

In the mosaic of your life, each piece—whether it's a fleeting moment or a significant event—holds the potential to contribute to the all-encompassing picture of who you are and what you stand for. Stoicism, with its rich heritage and profound insights, offers ageless principles that can help you mold these pieces into a coherent and meaningful whole. Integrating Stoic principles into your core beliefs isn't just about adopting a new way of thinking; it's about transforming your entire approach to life, ensuring that every decision and action resonates with philosophical harmony.

Imagine your core beliefs as the foundation of a building. Just as a strong foundation supports and stabilizes a structure, well-integrated core beliefs provide stability and direction in your life. Stoicism teaches that virtues such as wisdom, courage, justice, and temperance should form the bedrock of your foundation. These aren't just abstract concepts but practical guides that can steer your decisions and interactions. For instance, by embracing Stoic wisdom, you learn to see things as they really are, not as you wish them to be, leading to more realistic and grounded conclusions. Courage in Stoicism isn't just about heroic acts but about everyday bravery, such as standing up for what is right or admitting your mistakes.

Developing a personal ethical code based on Stoic virtues involves more than merely understanding these principles; it requires a commitment to live by them. This can start with small daily decisions—choosing honesty over deceit, patience over impulsiveness, or long-term good over short-term gain. Over time, these choices become habits, reinforcing your ethical code into your identity. Consider creating a personal "virtue manifesto," a written statement of the key Stoic virtues you aspire to live by, tailored to your individual goals and challenges. This manifesto can serve as a constant reminder and guide, helping you align your actions with your ethical framework, especially when faced with moral dilemmas or personal trials.

The beauty of Stoicism lies in its adaptability; it recognizes that life is diverse and ever-changing, and it allows for the flexibility to interpret its principles according to individual circumstances. This flexibility is crucial because it acknowledges that each person's life journey is unique. For example, the way you practice Stoic justice may seem different if you're a teacher, a parent, or a business leader, but the underlying principle—acting with fairness and consideration for others—remains the same. This adaptability urges you to personalize Stoic wisdom, making it relevant and applicable to your specific life situations, whether you're navigating career changes, personal relationships, or internal conflicts.

The transformative power of adopting a Stoic life philosophy is profound—it's about more than just coping with life's challenges; it's about thriving despite them. Stoicism equips you with tools to maintain inner peace in chaos, see growth in challenges, and foster harmony in relationships. It encourages a proactive approach to life, where you're not merely reacting to events but actively shaping your responses in line with your values. This proactive stance is empowering, instilling a sense of control and satisfaction that permeates all areas of life. As you continue to live out Stoic principles, you'll likely notice a shift in your overall well-being—a deeper sense of fulfillment, resilience against adversity, and a harmonious alignment with the world around you.

Embracing Stoicism as a life philosophy transforms everyday living into a more intentional and reflective practice, where each choice and action becomes proof of your values and beliefs. It fosters a life of purpose and integrity, where you're not just existing but truly living—guided by wisdom, driven by virtue, and fulfilled by the harmony between your beliefs and your actions. As you weave Stoic principles into the fabric of your life, you create a vibrant tapestry of experiences that not only reflects your true self but also contributes positively to the world around you.

STOICISM FOR LIFE TRANSITIONS AND NEW BEGINNINGS

Life, in its essence, is a series of transitions—each phase ushering in new challenges and opportunities. Whether it's stepping into a new career, moving to a different city, beginning or ending relationships, or other pivotal life events, these changes can be daunting. Stoicism, with its rich reservoir of wisdom, offers not just comfort but practical strategies for navigating these changes with poise and clarity.

Consider the profound impact of embracing Stoic virtues during these transitions. Courage, for instance, is not merely about boldly facing new challenges; it's about the subtle bravery of stepping into the unknown with hopefulness. It's about saying yes to a new job or a move across the country despite the uncertainties. Wisdom, another Stoic virtue, plays a critical role in making sound decisions during these times. It involves thoughtful consideration of the potential long-term effects of your choices, ensuring that your decisions align with your deepest values and long-term goals. Temperance, or the moderation of your desires and impulses, ensures that you maintain balance amidst the upheaval of change, preventing extreme reactions that might lead to regret.

The practical application of these principles is straightforward yet profound. For example, as you approach a significant career change, employ Stoic wisdom by thoroughly evaluating the new opportunity. Consider not only the financial and professional benefits but also how this change aligns with your values and long-term ambitions. Use temperance to balance your excitement with practicality, ensuring that your decision is well-rounded and sustainable. And let courage motivate you to take this step forward, even if it means leaving your comfort zone.

Strategies for Embracing New Beginnings with a Stoic Mindset

Adopting a Stoic mindset can be incredibly beneficial In effectively managing the uncertainties of new beginnings. Start by envisioning these changes as opportunities for growth rather than obstacles. This shift in perspective can significantly reduce anxiety and increase your openness to new experiences. Practically, this might involve setting clear, achievable goals for the transition period. For instance, if you are relocating, one of your goals could be to explore and connect with the community, which not only helps you to adapt to the new environment but also build a support system.

Another strategy is to maintain a Stoic journal during transitions. Regular entries allow you to reflect on your experiences, monitor your emotional and mental state, and assess how well you're aligning your actions with Stoic virtues. This practice not only provides clarity and direction but also serves as a record of your growth and adaptation through important life changes.

Stories of Stoic Adaptation

The practicality of Stoicism in navigating life's transitions is not just theoretical but is vividly illustrated in the lives of both historical and contemporary figures. Consider the story of Cato the Younger, a Roman politician known for his Stoic virtues. Facing the tumultuous political landscape of his time and the rise of Julius Caesar, Cato remained steadfast in his principles, demonstrating immense courage and integrity. His life serves as a profound example of how Stoic virtues can guide us through personal and societal upheavals.

In more recent times, consider the story of a modern executive who, after a sudden industry shift, found herself contemplating a significant career change. By applying Stoic principles, she navigated this transition with grace and foresight. She used wisdom to evaluate her options, courage to eventually start her consultancy, and temperance to maintain balance during the initial unstable months. Her success today is not just about her professional achievements but about her ability to maintain peace and satisfaction through life's unpredictable waves.

These stories not only inspire us but also demonstrate that Stoicism is as applicable in today's dynamic world as it was in ancient times. They show that Stoicism provides more than just a philosophical comfort; it offers practical tools that can help us navigate life's inevitable changes with confidence and wisdom.

Transitioning through life's various phases can indeed be challenging, but with Stoic principles as your guide, these become less about survival and more about flourishing. By embracing the virtues of courage, wisdom, and temperance and by viewing each change as an opportunity for growth, you equip yourself to handle new beginnings with a calm and optimistic mindset. This approach not only enhances your immediate adaptation but also contributes to a life of rich and fulfilling experiences marked by personal growth and resilience.

As we close this exploration of Stoicism for life transitions and new beginnings, remember that each change you face is not just a test of your ability to adapt but an opportunity to deepen your practice of Stoic virtues. These principles don't merely help you navigate changes; they transform how you experience them, turning each transition into a stepping stone towards a more virtuous and fulfilling life.

In the next chapter, we will explore how to maintain and deepen your Stoic practice over the long term, ensuring that Stoicism remains a vibrant and compelling part of your everyday life.

STOICISM IN THE DIGITAL AGE

In an era where the buzz of notifications and the glow of screens dominate much of our waking hours, how do we reclaim our attention and use our digital tools to enhance rather than detract from our lives? The ancient Stoics, who valued mastery over one's mind and impulses, offer a surprisingly relevant guide for navigating our modern digital landscape. This chapter will explore how you can apply Stoic discipline to handle digital distractions and enhance your focus, productivity, and peace of mind.

MANAGING DIGITAL DISTRACTIONS THROUGH STOIC DISCIPLINE

It is no secret that our digital devices, while incredibly useful, can also be sources of constant distraction. Social media notifications, the lure of endlessly scrolling through news feeds, and the rapid influx of emails can fragment our attention and lessen our ability to focus on the tasks and moments that truly matter. The challenge, then, is not just to use technology but to use it wisely and well.

The Stoic Principle of Control

Stoicism teaches us to distinguish between what we can control and what we cannot. In the context of digital distractions, this means recognizing that while we cannot control the design of apps or the strategies tech companies use to capture our attention, we can control our responses to these technologies. We have the power to choose where to direct our attention. This realization is the first step in reclaiming control over our digital interactions.

One effective Stoic exercise to enhance this aspect of control involves setting intentional times for checking emails or social media. For instance, rather than reacting to notifications as they arrive, you might decide to check your email only at set times during the day—perhaps once in the morning, once after lunch, and once before the end of your workday. This practice not only reduces the fragmentation of your attention but also allows you to engage with digital content more deliberately and effectively.

Creating a Disciplined Digital Environment

To further support your Stoic discipline in the digital realm, consider the physical and virtual environments in which you interact with technology. Decluttering your digital spaces can have a profound impact on your mental clarity and ability to focus. Start by organizing your digital files and uninstalling apps that you no longer use, or that tend to waste your time. Utilize technology tools that limit usage or block distracting websites during work hours to help maintain your focus.

Additionally, creating physical boundaries for device use can be incredibly helpful. Designate specific areas of your home, such as the bedroom or dining room, as tech-free zones. This not only helps reduce digital distractions but also promotes better sleep and more meaningful interactions with family members.

Stoic Mindfulness in Digital Engagements

Another powerful Stoic practice involves using moments of digital engagement as opportunities to practice self-control and mindfulness. Before opening an app or responding to an email, take a moment to breathe deeply and remind yourself of your intention for this interaction. Ask yourself: Is this action necessary? Is it aligned with my values and goals? By pausing to reflect in this way, you transform a potentially mindless reaction into a mindful action.

Visual Element: The Stoic Digital Discipline Flowchart

To aid in applying these principles, consider the Stoic Digital Discipline Flowchart—an infographic that outlines a step-by-step process to manage digital distractions effectively. This flowchart prompts you to ask key questions before engaging with digital technology, helping you make more deliberate and controlled use of your devices. It serves as a visual reminder of the Stoic principles discussed in this section, integrating ancient wisdom with modern challenges to help you navigate your digital life with greater purpose and tranquility.

SOCIAL MEDIA AND STOICISM: MAINTAINING EMOTIONAL EQUANIMITY ONLINE

In the vast, interconnected web of social media, it's easy to fall into the trap of constant comparison, where every post and update from others can seem like a reflection of what we lack. This digital landscape, brimming with curated realities showcasing perfect lives, can significantly skew our perception, leading to feelings of inadequacy, envy, or even anger. Yet, through the lens of Stoicism, we find valuable strategies to navigate this space more mindfully, ensuring that our engagement with social media enriches rather than depletes us.

Stoic Wisdom on Emotional Detachment

The Stoic practice of emotional detachment offers a powerful antidote to the negative impacts of social media. By focusing on internal values rather than external validation, Stoicism teaches us to cultivate indifference to things that lie outside our moral purpose. This doesn't mean we should adopt a callous or disconnected attitude; instead, we should choose to anchor our self-worth in our own virtues and actions rather than in the approval of others. For instance, when encountering a post that triggers feelings of jealousy or inadequacy, a Stoic approach would involve a conscious shift of focus from external measures of success—like wealth or physical appearance—to personal progress and ethical integrity. This shift not only alleviates distressing emotions but also aligns our social media interactions with our deeper values, fostering a sense of contentment and self-respect.

Mindful Engagement with Social Media

To further enhance our experience online, Stoicism encourages the practice of mindfulness, particularly in how we engage with social media. This involves being acutely aware of our emotional state before, during, and after our digital interactions. By examining ourselves prior to scrolling through social media, we can better understand our motivations—are we seeking connection, distraction, or validation? During our engagement, maintaining this awareness helps us notice when feelings of distress or comparison begin to surface, allowing us to pause and realign with our Stoic principles. Afterward, reflecting on our feelings can inform whether our interaction was beneficial or if adjustments are needed in our future engagements. This mindful approach transforms our social media use from a passive and potentially harmful activity into an opportunity for personal growth and self-awareness.

Stoic Reflections on Social Media Interactions

Regular reflection on our interactions with social media is a critical Stoic practice that can significantly enhance our online experiences. By taking time to assess whether our engagements are contributing positively to our lives, we can make informed decisions about how best to use these powerful tools. This might involve setting boundaries around the time spent online, curating our feeds to include more positive and inspiring content, or even taking periodic breaks from social media to reconnect with our offline lives. Such reflections not only help in maintaining emotional balance but also ensure that our digital habits align with our overall goals and values, reinforcing our Stoic commitment to living a virtuous life.

In practicing these Stoic strategies—emotional detachment, mindful engagement, and regular reflection—we not only protect ourselves from the potential downsides of social media but also harness its capabilities to support our personal and spiritual growth. These practices empower us to navigate the digital realm with wisdom and composure, turning every scroll or click into a step toward greater self-understanding and equanimity.

APPLYING STOICISM TO ONLINE INTERACTIONS AND RELATIONSHIPS

In the vast expanse of the digital world, our interactions often lack the physical and emotional cues that guide our communications in person. This absence can sometimes lead to less empathetic and more impulsive exchanges, where the anonymity and physical detachment of online platforms may encourage behaviors and statements that we might shy away from in face-to-face settings. The veil of a screen can embolden some to express harsher criticisms or engage in more confrontational dialogue than they usually would. Understanding these dynamics is crucial in applying Stoic principles to navigate online environments effectively.

The Stoic virtues—justice, temperance, and courage—are not just ideals for personal development but are immensely practical in enhancing online interactions. Justice, in a Stoic sense, involves treating others fairly and with kindness, an approach that is often challenged in the faceless interactions of the internet. To embody Stoic justice online, remember that behind every profile picture and username is an actual person with real feelings, challenges, and a life as complex as your own. This understanding can temper our responses, ensuring they are not just truthful but also considerate and constructive.

Temperance, or moderation, is another virtue that is vital in the digital realm. It guides us to respond to others—not with impulsive reactions—but with measured, thoughtful words. Applying temperance can mean taking a moment to breathe and reflect before replying to a provocative comment or choosing not to engage in every debate you encounter online. This not only helps maintain your peace of mind but also fosters a more constructive online environment. For instance, if you experience a heated debate within a social media group, choosing to provide a balanced, well-thought-out response, or sometimes choosing not to engage at all, can be a demonstration of temperance.

The virtue of courage, which in Stoicism involves not just bravery in the face of physical danger but also the moral courage to speak and live truthfully, is particularly relevant when we consider the spread of misinformation online. Exhibiting Stoic courage can mean standing up for truth and integrity by fact-checking information before sharing it or by respectfully correcting misconceptions in online discussions. It requires bravery to maintain your ethical standards even when it might be easier or more comfortable to blend into the consensus and stay silent.

Guidelines for Virtuous Online Behavior

It's helpful to establish clear personal guidelines rooted in Stoic virtues in order to maintain decorum and respect in online discussions, especially when faced with challenging interactions such as dealing with internet trolls. First, always aim to communicate with respect and sincerity, keeping in mind that your words have the power to affect others deeply. When encountering trolls or overly aggressive commenters, a Stoic approach would involve responding with calmness and logic or choosing not to engage at all, thereby not allowing such interactions to disturb your peace.

Creating a positive impact in digital communities can also involve actively contributing to discussions that foster understanding and shared learning. Share insights, offer support, and express appreciation for valuable contributions from others. These actions not only enrich the community but also strengthen your practice of Stoic virtues by focusing on constructive and meaningful exchanges.

Moreover, the role of community in Stoicism is profoundly significant. Modern online platforms can serve as contemporary Stoic communities where individuals seek advice, find support, and share wisdom. Participating in or even forming online groups focused on Stoic philosophy and its application in daily life can provide valuable opportunities for learning and growth. These communities allow for the exchange of ideas and experiences that can deepen understanding and inspire the practical application of Stoic principles in diverse aspects of life.

Navigating the digital world through the lens of Stoicism equips you not only to handle the challenges of online interactions but to transform these experiences into opportunities for personal growth and positive contributions. The practice of these ancient virtues on modern platforms demonstrates the timeless relevance of Stoic wisdom, guiding us to lead more thoughtful, balanced, and meaningful digital lives.

THE MODERN STOIC: INTEGRATING ANCIENT
WISDOM IN A HIGH-TECH WORLD

In an age where technology permeates every aspect of our lives, the challenge often lies not in adopting new technologies but in integrating them in ways that enhance our well-being rather than detract from it. The ancient practice of Stoicism, with its focus on wisdom, virtue, and self-control, offers valuable insights into how we can use modern technologies, such as digital apps and virtual reality, to deepen our understanding and practice of these timeless principles.

The adaptation of traditional Stoic practices, such as journaling and meditation, to modern technologies is not just a matter of convenience but also enhances accessibility and engagement. For instance, digital journaling apps can ease the Stoic practice of daily reflection by making it easier to track thoughts, emotions, and actions over time. These apps often come with features like reminders and prompts, which can help you maintain consistency in your reflective practices. Similarly, virtual reality offers new dimensions to meditation, allowing you to immerse yourself in serene environments that might not be manageable in your daily surroundings. This can be particularly beneficial in cultivating the Stoic practice of mindfulness and presence, as these immersive experiences can help you detach from everyday distractions and focus intensely on your internal state.

Moreover, the benefits of technology in practicing Stoicism also extend to educational and community aspects. Many apps are dedicated to Stoicism and provide daily meditations, quotes from Stoic philosophers, and interactive exercises that make the philosophy more accessible and applicable to everyday life. These digital platforms not only serve as tools for individual practice but also foster a sense of community among those interested in Stoicism. Users can share insights, discuss interpretations of Stoic texts, and support each other in applying Stoic principles to modern challenges. This communal aspect is crucial, as Stoicism emphasizes not only personal growth but also the development of virtues that contribute to the welfare of society.

However, the incorporation of Stoicism into our high-tech world is not without its challenges. The rapid pace of digital interactions and the often superficial nature of online communications can seem at odds with the profound, reflective nature of Stoic philosophy. Here, the Stoic practice of mindfulness becomes especially relevant. By consciously slowing down our interactions with technology—pausing to reflect on the purpose and impact of our digital engagements—we can counteract the frenetic pace of the digital age. This might involve setting intentions before using technology, such as seeking to learn something new or connecting meaningfully with others rather than mindlessly scrolling through content.

Encouraging a balanced approach to technology is also essential. Stoicism teaches us to use external things without becoming dependent on them, a principle that can guide our use of technology. It's about leveraging technology to enhance our lives and virtues without letting it dictate our happiness or self-worth. For example, while a Stoic app might help you practice mindfulness, it's essential also to cultivate the ability to be mindful without it, ensuring that your practice is grounded in internal skills rather than external aids.

In embracing these strategies, you align with the Stoic ideal of living according to nature. In today's terms, this can be interpreted as living in harmony with the technological environment that surrounds us—using it thoughtfully and purposefully to enhance our capacity for virtue, wisdom, and contentment. By doing so, you not only navigate the high-tech world more effectively but also deepen your practice of Stoicism, finding in ancient wisdom a powerful partner for modern living.

As we conclude this exploration of integrating Stoicism in the digital age, we see how ancient practices can find new expressions and applications in modern settings. This chapter has shown that by adapting Stoic wisdom to contemporary tools, we can enhance our understanding and application of this philosophical tradition, making it even more relevant and valuable in our daily lives. The next chapter will focus on consolidating these practices into a cohesive Stoic lifestyle, ensuring that the principles of Stoicism are not just something we study but something we live, day by day.

CONCLUSION

As we draw the curtains on this journey through the enriching landscape of Stoicism, it's essential to reflect on the transformative power this ancient philosophy holds for our modern lives. Stoicism isn't merely a set of theories confined to dusty old tomes; it's a vibrant, practical guide that offers enduring wisdom for navigating today's world with its rapid changes, overwhelming choices, and unprecedented challenges.

Throughout this book, we've explored how Stoicism can help us manage stress, engage more mindfully with technology, cultivate robust relationships, and foster personal growth. Each chapter has not only delved into Stoic principles but has also connected these age-old ideas to contemporary issues—whether in dealing with digital distractions, enhancing emotional intelligence, or navigating complex social dynamics.

Key Takeaways: Remember, adopting Stoicism is about more than understanding its philosophy; it's about living it. The core Stoic virtues—wisdom, courage, justice, and temperance—can guide your daily decisions and interactions. By practicing mindfulness, engaging in daily reflections, and approaching life's challenges with a Stoic mindset, you can cultivate a life of peace, resilience, and fulfillment.

Call to Action: I urge you, the reader, to not view this as the end but as the beginning of your Stoic practice. Start with small, manageable steps. Integrate moments of reflection into your morning routine, practice mindfulness throughout your day, and challenge yourself to respond to life's complexities with Stoic calm and rationality. These practices are not meant to be temporary fixes but parts of a lifelong journey toward more profound wisdom and greater virtue.

Join the Stoic Community: You are not alone on this path. The Stoic community, both online and possibly in your local area, offers a network of support and friendship. Engage with forums, participate in discussions, and attend Stoic meetings and events. Sharing your journey with others can provide not only inspiration but also fresh perspectives that enrich your understanding of Stoicism.

Encourage Personal Exploration: I urge you to dive deeper into the texts of Marcus Aurelius, Seneca, and Epictetus, among others. Each Stoic philosopher offers unique insights that you might find resonate differently with your personal experiences and challenges. Remember, Stoicism is highly personal, and its application can be tailored to fit your individual life circumstances and values.

Acknowledge the Ongoing Nature of Stoic Practice: Embrace the fact that Stoicism is a path, not a destination. It is a philosophy of ongoing practice and continual growth. There will be setbacks and challenges, but each is an opportunity to apply Stoic principles and learn from the experience.

Finally, I want to express my heartfelt gratitude to you for joining me in exploring the profound and practical world of Stoicism. May this book serve as a steadfast companion as you navigate the complexities of modern life. Approach each day with Stoic wisdom and serenity, and remember that every moment is an opportunity to live according to your highest virtues.

Thank you for embarking on this journey towards a Stoic life. May you find in Stoicism the strength, peace, and joy that I have discovered.

REFERENCES

What is Stoicism? The Basics of The World's Greatest ... https://orionphilosophy.com/stoicism-meaning-and-definition/

Zeno of Citium | Stoic, Cynic, Founder https://www.britannica.com/biography/Zeno-of-Citium

Mastering Modern Life with Stoic Philosophy: 10 Insights and ... https://thegeekyleader.com/2024/01/07/mastering-modern-life-with-stoic-philosophy-10-insights-and-practical-applications/#:

How to be a Modern Stoic: Stoicism in the 21st Century https://mindandpractice.com/how-to-be-a-modern-stoic-stoicism-in-the-21st-century/

Best Quotes from Seneca's Letters from a Stoic https://www.getstoic.com/quotes/best-quotes-seneca-letters-from-a-stoic

How To Plan Your Day Like Marcus Aurelius https://dailystoic.com/marcus-aurelius-daily-habits/

Epictetus on Freedom, Thinking, Information and ... https://fs.blog/the-art-of-living/

Why Stoicism Is More Relevant Than You Might Think https://www.psychologytoday.com/us/blog/365-ways-to-be-more-stoic/202301/why-stoicism-is-more-relevant-than-you-might-think

Beginners Guide to Stoicism https://modernstoicism.com/beginners-guide-to-stoicism/

Modern Stoicism: How To Use Ancient ... https://orionphilosophy.com/stoic-philosophy-for-modern-life/

A Stoic's 9-Minute Micro Morning Routine For Guaranteed ... https://medium.com/mind-cafe/a-stoics-9-minute-micro-morning-routine-a86e87e7101d

Resilience: Build skills to endure hardship https://www.mayoclinic.org/tests-procedures/resilience-training/in-depth/resilience/art-20046311

The Stoic Dichotomy of Control in Practice https://www.psychologytoday.com/us/blog/365-ways-to-be-more-stoic/202304/the-stoic-dichotomy-of-control-in-practice

Cognitive Restructuring Techniques for Reframing Thoughts https://positivepsychology.com/cbt-cognitive-restructuring-cognitive-distortions/

21 Mindfulness Exercises & Activities For Adults (+ PDF) https://positivepsychology.com/mindfulness-exercises-techniques-activities/

Famous Stoics in History and Pop Culture | Living By Example https://www.livingbyexample.org/famous-stoics-in-history-and-pop-culture/

Stoicism for Conflict Resolution: Use Stoic Philosophy to ... https://www.stoicsimple. com/stoicism-for-conflict-resolution-use-stoic-philosophy-to-resolve-conflicts/

What Stoic Philosophy Says About Love | by Wesley Owens https://medium.com/love-the-magazine/what-stoic-philosophy-says-about-love-913bb82c416d

Communication & Stoicism: How to Communicate Better with Stoic Philosophy https:// www.stoicsimple.com/communication-stoicism-how-to-communicate-better-with-stoic-philosophy/#:

Stoic advice: what do Stoics think of forgiveness? https://howtobeastoic.wordpress. com/2017/04/22/stoic-advice-what-do-stoics-think-of-forgiveness/

How to Let Go of Anger: Seneca's 16 Stoic Techniques https://www.highexistence.com/ seneca-on-how-to-deal-with-anger/

Stoicism and Envy: Using Stoic Philosophy to Deal With ... https://www.stoicsimple. com/stoicism-and-envy-using-stoic-philosophy-to-deal-with-jealousy/#:

How to Cope With Fear and Anxiety, the Stoic Way https://www.psychologytoday. com/us/blog/hide-and-seek/202203/how-to-cope-with-fear-and-anxiety-the-stoic-way

Benefits Of Adopting A Stoic Mindset In Your Work And Life https://www.forbes.com/ sites/jackkelly/2024/04/12/benefits-of-stoicism/#:

A Stoic Response to Grief https://dailystoic.com/stoic-response-grief/

The Stoic Resilience of James Stockdale - The Will Project https://willproject.org/exam ples/stoic-resilience-stockdale/

How Stoicism Perfectly Helps You Deal With Change https://orionphilosophy.com/ stoicism-change/

MODERN STOICISM AND ITS USEFULNESS IN ... https://www.crisisjournal.org/ api/v1/articles/33608-modern-stoicism-and-its-usefulness-in-fostering-resilience.pdf

Cognitive Behavior Therapy - StatPearls https://www.ncbi.nlm.nih.gov/ books/NBK470241/

Mindfulness exercises - Mayo Clinic https://www.mayoclinic.org/healthy-lifestyle/ consumer-health/in-depth/mindfulness-exercises/art-20046356

The empirical status of acceptance and commitment therapy https://www.sciencedirect. com/science/article/pii/S2212144720301940

Road to resilience: a systematic review and meta-analysis ... https://bmjopen.bmj.com/ content/8/6/e017858

Eudaimonia https://www.thestoicregistry.org/res/pathways/eudaimonia/

Stoicism vs. Hedonism: What's the Difference? https://orionphilosophy.com/stoicism-vs-hedonism/

10 Insanely Useful Stoic Exercises https://dailystoic.com/10-insanely-useful-stoic-exercises/

5 Epic Leaders Who Studied Stoicism -- and Why You ... https://www.entrepreneur.com/leadership/5-epic-leaders-who-studied-stoicism-and-why-you-should/252625

The Stoic Paradoxes - Stoic Compass - WordPress.com https://stoiccompass.wordpress.com/2017/10/20/the-stoic-paradoxes/

An Ancient Stoic Meditation Technique https://donaldrobertson.name/2017/03/22/an-ancient-stoic-meditation-technique/

6 Stoicism and Modern Virtue Ethics - Oxford Academic https://academic.oup.com/book/44871/chapter/384583553

10 Stoic Habits for Maintaining Work-Life Balance https://thegeekyleader.com/2024/05/26/10-stoic-habits-for-maintaining-work-life-balance/

How To Practice Stoicism: An Introduction & 12 ... https://mindfulstoic.net/how-to-practice-stoicism-an-introduction-12-stoic-practices/

A Daily Regimen for the Modern Stoic | by PocketStoic Staff https://medium.com/pocketstoic/a-daily-regimen-for-the-modern-stoic-e4b9ae750e58

The Modern Application of Stoic Philosophy in Daily Life https://stoicstateuniversity.com/blog/the-modern-application-of-stoic-philosophy-in-daily-life

How Stoicism Perfectly Helps You Deal With Change https://orionphilosophy.com/stoicism-change/

Stoic Principles in the Digital Age: A Guide to Digital Detox https://medium.com/@m.daudup25/stoic-principles-in-the-digital-age-a-guide-to-digital-detox-aed25905b650

The Stoics were right – emotional control is good for the soul https://psyche.co/ideas/the-stoics-were-right-emotional-control-is-good-for-the-soul

Managing Social Media Stress with Mindfulness https://childmind.org/article/social-media-stress-mindfulness/

A Daily Regimen for the Modern Stoic | by PocketStoic Staff https://medium.com/pocketstoic/a-daily-regimen-for-the-modern-stoic-e4b9ae750e58

www.ingramcontent.com/pod-product-compliance
Lightning Source LLC
Chambersburg PA
CBHW060236030426
42335CB00014B/1477